THIS BOOK IS THE PROPERTY OF:

Elkhart Christian
Academy
education impacting hearts

25943 CR 22 East • Elkhart, IN 46517
p: 574.293.1609   f: 574.293.3238
www.elkhartchristian.org

The fact that this volume appears in our library does not mean that Elkhart Christian Academy necessarily endorses everything it says about morals, philosophy, theology, or science. The position of the school is that these things must be interpreted in the light of the Scriptures. The Bible gives us our standards in all areas of life.

LAYMAN'S LIBRARY OF CHRISTIAN DOCTRINE

The Holy Spirit

WAYNE E. WARD

BROADMAN PRESS
Nashville, Tennessee

4216-40

ISBN: 0-8054-1640-4

Dewey Decimal Classification: 231.3

Subject Heading: HOLY SPIRIT

Library of Congress Catalog Card Number: 86-14709

Printed in the United States of America

Library of Congress Cataloging-in-Publication Data

Ward, Wayne E.
  The Holy Spirit.

  (Layman's library of Christian doctrine; 10)
  Includes index.
  1. Holy Spirit. I. Title. II. Series.
BT121.2.W33 1987   231'.3   86-14709
ISBN 0-8054-1640-4

Foreword

The *Layman's Library of Christian Doctrine* in sixteen volumes covers the major doctrines of the Christian faith.

To meet the needs of the lay reader, the *Library* is written in a popular style. Headings are used in each volume to help the reader understand which part of the doctrine is being dealt with. Technical terms, if necessary to the discussion, will be clearly defined.

The need for this series is evident. Christians need to have a theology of their own, not one handed to them by someone else. The *Library* is written to help readers evaluate and form their own beliefs based on the Bible and on clear and persuasive statements of historic Christian positions. The aim of the series is to help laymen hammer out their own personal theology.

The books range in size from 140 pages to 168 pages. Each volume deals with a major part of Christian doctrine. Although some overlap is unavoidable, each volume will stand on its own. A set of the sixteen-volume series will give a person a complete look at the major doctrines of the Christian church.

Each volume is personalized by its author. The author will show the vitality of Christian doctrines and their meaning for everyday life. Strong and fresh illustrations will hold the interest of the reader. At times the personal faith of the authors will be seen in illustrations from their own Christian pilgrimage.

Not all laymen are aware they are theologians. Many may believe they know nothing of theology. However, every person believes something. This series helps the layman to understand what he believes and to be able to be "prepared to make a defense to anyone who calls him to account for the hope that is in him" (1 Pet. 3:15, RSV).

Contents

Introduction

"God is spirit." This statement of Jesus in John 4:24 means that everything we say about God must be related in some way to spirit. It means invisible rather than visible. It means that we cannot relate to God as matter that we can touch or see or measure. The scientific principles that govern all our experience and education in today's world cannot be applied to God.

But this fact has opened the door to a jungle of confusion and strange cults regarding the Spirit of God. If we cannot depend upon science and human reason to provide our understanding of the Spirit, what can we depend upon? The Christian answer is clear and unmistakable: We must follow the teaching of Jesus as revealed in Holy Scripture. Just as Jesus revealed to us the Father, so He also revealed to us the Holy Spirit. Any spirit which does not magnify and exalt Jesus is not the Spirit of God.

Spirit in the Old Testament

Because all of our understanding of the Holy Spirit goes back to the biblical witness, we must look first at the activity of the Spirit in the Old Testament.[1] Some Christians have assumed that the Holy Spirit began on the Day of Pentecost, when the early church was empowered by the Spirit to proclaim the gospel of Christ. But what happened at Pentecost can be compared to what happened at Bethlehem. Jesus did not become the Son of God by being born of Mary in Bethlehem. The Son was with the Father from all eternity. Otherwise, He could not be the divine Son of God. He became *flesh and blood* through His birth to Mary. The eternal Son of God became the man Jesus through Mary.

In a parallel way, the Holy Spirit came to indwell the body of the church through the outpouring at Pentecost. Like the Son, the Spirit had been with the Father from all eternity. He was hovering over the great deep in creation (Gen. 1:2). But this eternal Spirit of God found a dwelling place in the body of Christ, the church. Pentecost was to the Spirit what Bethlehem was to the Son—the place of incarnation or embodiment of the Son and the Spirit for their ministry in the world.

The primary role of the Spirit in the Old Testament was in creation.[2] He was present in the creative activity of God in Genesis 1, and Psalm 104 shows that the Spirit keeps the created order alive and functioning. In this role the Spirit does not have a particular dwelling place but rather permeates the whole of creation at all times.

This is very different from the New Testament where the Holy Spirit dwells specifically in Jesus in His redemptive ministry, empowering His miracles and His words, and then indwells the church, which continues the ministry of Christ in the world. There is also a *redemptive* role of the Holy Spirit in the Old Testament. He brought the powerful word of God through the prophets, and He moved through the wind to roll the waters back and deliver God's people from death. But in these activities in the Old Testament, the Spirit was coming and going. He did not have a permanent dwelling place. This is a significant difference in the role of the Holy Spirit in the Old Testament and in the New.

Tracing the activity of the Holy Spirit through the Torah, or Pentateuch, the first five books of the Hebrew canon of

Scripture is an exciting journey. The Spirit who was active in creation became the powerful presence of God leading His people out of slavery, in the Exodus, and guiding them to the Promised Land. The Spirit was active in forming and preserving the covenant of God with His people.

In the second division of the Hebrew canon of Scripture, we have the activity of the Spirit of God in the prophets. He inspired and empowered the word of God through the prophets to the people. The work of the Holy Spirit in the prophetic canon of Scripture was primarily redemptive activity, bringing the saving word of God to the people and convicting them of their sin. But, in the background, we still see the creative activity of God's Spirit in the whole universe and to all the peoples of the earth. The twofold work of the Spirit came to focus on both creation and redemption.

In the Psalms and the Writings, the third and final division of the Hebrew Bible, the creative role of the Spirit in sustaining the whole universe is still very prominent. But a new dimension of His activity came to the fore, that was His personal work in the heart and mind of the worshiper. In the Psalms, in particular, the Holy Spirit was the powerful presence of God in the life of the individual worshiper. This emphasis upon the personal ministry of the Spirit anticipated and prepared the way for the work of the Holy Spirit in the life of the Christian believer. The fundamental difference is that in the New Testament the Holy Spirit had the redemptive ministry of Jesus as the basis for His convicting and regenerating work in the life of the Christian believer. Because of the atoning work of Jesus, the Holy Spirit in the New Testament was able to regenerate the life of the believer and empower him to share with others the new life in Christ.

Spirit in the New Testament

Unlike the Old Testament, where the Spirit of God came and went, the Spirit came upon Jesus and stayed. Jesus was begotten by the Holy Spirit through the virgin Mary; He was anointed with the Spirit at His baptism; by the Spirit of God Jesus cast out demons; Jesus gave up His Spirit as He died on the cross and was raised up from the dead by the Holy Spirit. The entire life of Jesus was an embodiment of the Holy Spirit. The anointing of Jesus by the Spirit at His baptism for His messianic mission is exactly what the name *Christ* (or *Messiah*) means: the Anointed One! The fullness of the Godhead, Father, Son, and Spirit, was embodied in Jesus.

Jesus and the Holy Spirit

Careful study of all of the Gospels is necessary to see how the Holy Spirit lived and worked through the life of Jesus. This study will focus especially upon Jesus' conception and birth, and then it will trace His development "in wisdom, and stature, and in favor with God and man" (Luke 2:52).

The crucial role of the Spirit in anointing Jesus at His baptism for His messianic ministry will lead us to a careful study of the activity of the Holy Spirit in the teaching and the miracles of Jesus. Just as we learn about God the Father from the intimate relationship of Jesus to His Father in His prayer life, so we come to understand the power of the Holy Spirit in the miracles Jesus performed.

The Paraclete

By far the most important Scriptures for understanding the relationship of Father, Son, and Holy Spirit will be the five Paraclete hymns, or sayings, in John's Gospel. These beautiful verses, probably sung in the early church, spell out the relationship of Jesus to the Spirit-Paraclete and the relationship of the Spirit to the Father and the Son. We learn more about the personality and the ministry of the Holy Spirit from these words than from any others in the Bible. We will see that the Son bears witness to the Father and that the Spirit bears witness to the Son. This sequence and relationship are crucial for understanding the activity of the Holy Spirit in our lives today.

The Holy Spirit in the Church

When Jesus returned to the right hand of the Father, the Holy Spirit was poured out upon Jesus' band of followers in order that they might continue His ministry in the world. The Book of Acts records this thrilling story. For this reason, Acts is sometimes called the "gospel of the Holy Spirit." Even as the Gospels record the redemptive ministry of Jesus, empowered by the Holy Spirit, so Acts continues the story of that redemptive ministry in the church, empowered by the same Holy Spirit. We are continuing in that same ministry in the church today, and we are completely dependent upon the power of the Holy Spirit to accomplish our mission in the world. If Jesus needed to pray and depend upon the empowering of the Spirit in His ministry, how much more must we rely upon the Holy Spirit to empower us?

The Holy Spirit in the Life of the Christian

Even as the Holy Spirit fills the church for its ministry in the world, the individual Christian must be filled with the Spirit for a victorious life in the world. The very word *filling* is often used to describe the way in which the Spirit comes into the life of the believer to empower that life for service. Sometimes the phrase "baptism of the Holy Spirit" is used to describe the coming of the Spirit into the life of the believer. We need to discover exactly what this means in the New Testament and how it is related to the "filling" of the Spirit.[3]

Some of the deepest misunderstandings in the church today come about because of confusion over the "baptism of the Spirit," the "filling of the Holy Spirit," and "the gifts of the Spirit."

The writings of Paul, in particular, emphasize the gifts of the Holy Spirit to the church and in the lives of the individual members. While these spiritual gifts undoubtedly bring joy and fulfillment to the individual believer, Paul stressed their role in building up and strengthening the church. They are not private gifts in which the Christian may glory; rather, they are God's gift to the church, for His glory. Much of the confusion and conflict in the church today over the gifts of the Spirit would be corrected if this primary emphasis of Paul were remembered. They are corporate gifts, given for the edification and blessing of the whole church, not for private enjoyment.

The Spirit is the "earnest and seal" of our final redemption at the coming of the Lord and the resurrection of the body. The presence of the Spirit in the life of the Christian is already a foretaste of the life to come; at the same time, this gives the seal and assurance the believer needs until faith becomes sight. This is another great emphasis of the apostle Paul, and it has brought strength and blessing to suffering Christians down through the centuries. By the eyes of the Spirit, they have already been able to see the end of the journey. Christians know that the suffering of this present time is not even to be compared to the glory that shall be revealed when Jesus comes.

The Spirit of Christ

Some misunderstanding of the Holy Spirit has come about through the effort to distinguish between the Spirit of God and the Spirit of Christ, making two different spirits in the being of God. The unity of God is the absolutely fundamental doctrine of the being of God, and all such efforts to separate God into different beings, even spiritual beings, would result in the destruction of the most precious doctrine of all: "Hear, O Israel: The Lord our God is one Lord" (Deut. 6:4).

This unity makes impossible some of the doctrines proclaimed today which sharply separate Christ from the Spirit. For instance, see 2 Corinthians 3:17. Some teach that one may have Christ, or be saved by Christ, but not have the Holy Spirit until later, or not at all. The Scriptures simply do not allow the splitting of the being of God in this fashion. The Father, Son, and Holy Spirit are all involved in the work of regeneration and redemption because all are one. There is no activity of any of the persons of the Trinity which is in isolation from the others. Otherwise, the unity of God would be destroyed.

The Regenerating Spirit

Just as the Spirit of God was active in the creation of the world, so He is active in the new creation, the regeneration of the individual believer. Every born-again believer knows that it takes a miracle of God to transform life and make a new creature. No amount of human effort can accomplish this, and no adequate explanation can leave out the supernatural power of the Holy Spirit.

For this reason, any proper understanding of the doctrine of the Holy Spirit compels us to acknowledge the reality of miracle. Only a power above and beyond us can account for the creation of the whole universe, and only such a supernatural power can sustain the whole creation at any moment. In a parallel way, only the suprahuman power of the Holy Spirit can recreate the human life and make it over again in the renewed image of God. Some people fail to see the miraculous nature of the new birth and concentrate instead on miracles of physical healing or material blessing. These miracles may be more visible to those who are only spectators, but the genuine believer knows that there is no greater miracle than the new birth.

The Empowering Spirit

Just as Jesus was begotten by the Holy Spirit and then later was anointed by the Holy Spirit for His mission as Messiah, so those believers who are born again by the Holy Spirit must be continually filled and empowered by the Spirit for their lives of service in the world. The *baptism* of the Holy Spirit is always closely connected with the beginning of the Christian journey, with regeneration and water baptism. It is a once-for-all experience, never repeated in the life of the believer. On the other hand, the "filling" of the Holy Spirit or the anointing of the Spirit may be often repeated and may even enable the Christian to perform a particular task for the Lord.

There has been so much conflict over the doctrines of the baptism of the Spirit, over the claims of a second blessing or "work of grace," and over the gift of tongues as a sign of this spiritual baptism that some have turned away entirely from any serious study of the ministry of the Holy Spirit in their Christian lives. That reaction is tragic. The conflict calls for more careful study of the biblical teachings and more experience of the Holy Spirit in our lives. This book is an effort to lead us through an intensive study of the person and ministry of the Holy Spirit because that is the best way to clear up the confusion and to lead us to a deeper experience of the Holy Spirit in our own lives. This study will major upon the biblical texts which teach us about the Spirit of God, seeking to apply them to the understanding and enrichment of our lives in the Spirit today.

Notes

1. The classic treatment of the Holy Spirit in the biblical tradition is a work by Irving F. Wood, *The Spirit of God in Biblical Literature* (London: Hodder and Stoughton, 1904), 280 pp. But most of the more recent works begin with the Old Testament emphasis and trace the development through the Bible: Alasdair I. C. Heron, *The Holy Spirit* (Philadelphia: The Westminster Press, 1983), 212 pp; Dale Moody, *Spirit of the Living God* (Philadelphia: The Westminster Press, 1968), 239 pp.; George T. Montague, S.M., *The Holy Spirit: Growth of a Biblical Tradition* (New York: Paulist Press, 1976), 374 pp.

2. See this emphasis in Regin Prenter, *Spiritus Creator,* John M. Jensen, trans. (Philadelphia: Muhlenberg Press, 1953), esp. p. 184 *ff.*

3. A thorough treatment of this distinction between "baptism" and "filling" of the Spirit is found in Frederick Dale Bruner, *A Theology of the Holy Spirit* (Grand Rapids: William B. Eerdmans, 1970), 390 pp.

1

The Holy Spirit in the Pentateuch

"In the beginning God . . ." (Gen. 1:1). This is exactly how far back we have to go when we begin a study of the Holy Spirit. He was at the beginning of creation and before. Just as God *was* before anything was created, so the Spirit *was* in the being of God from all eternity.

The second verse of the Bible records the very first reference to the Spirit: "The Spirit of God was moving over the face of the waters" (Gen. 1:2). The Hebrew word translated "moving" literally means "hovering" or "brooding" like a bird over its nest. Something was about to come forth out of "the deep" by the mighty power of God's Spirit, which was brooding over it. This first reference to the birdlike brooding of the Spirit may support the biblical imagery of the Holy Spirit as a dove. Until this day the doves hover on the wing over the Jordan Valley, hardly moving their position for hours. We can easily see the appropriateness of the Holy Spirit coming down upon Jesus like a dove at His baptism in the Jordan River.

The word *Spirit* is *ruach* in Hebrew and means "wind," as well as "spirit."[1] This does not mean that God's Spirit is literally wind because wind is air in motion, a part of God's created world. God's Spirit is the Creator who made the wind—and all other created things. But it does mean that the common word for "wind" was a good word to describe or name the invisible but powerful activity of God. Like the wind, God's Spirit is powerful and invisible. We cannot see the Spirit any more than we can see the wind, but we can see or experience the effects of the Spirit, as we experience the effects of the wind.

The Universal Spirit

No theme permeates the Bible more completely than the power and presence of the Holy Spirit of God. Just as we encounter a direct reference to the Holy Spirit in the second verse of the Bible, so we have the Spirit in the closing verses of the Bible: "The Spirit and the Bride say, 'Come'" (Rev. 22:17).

In dealing with the topic of the Holy Spirit, we are not simply considering one separate theological doctrine. We are considering the omnipresent God Himself. We are searching for the Reality and Person of the Living God, in whom we live and move and have our being.[2] Our attitude must be one of humble worship and praise, for we can never comprehend or understand Him fully with our limited minds. What we can do is learn more about the Person and activity of the Holy Spirit as revealed in the Scriptures, especially in the life and ministry of Jesus. In this way we can learn more about surrendering our lives to the Holy Spirit in order that He may live and work through us.

We dare not relegate the doctrine of the Spirit to a single article in a creed or confession of faith. The Spirit permeates every aspect of our life of faith, and no Christian doctrine is complete without Him. He is the Breath which gives life to every Christian doctrine, from the convicting power which brings us to salvation to the resurrection of the spiritual body and the life everlasting. We will find it impossible to treat thoroughly any Christian doctrine without examining the role of the Holy Spirit in that particular aspect of the Christian life. A full analysis of the Person and ministry of the Holy Spirit will, in a similar way, touch on every aspect of the Christian life. The Spirit is truly universal. He is present everywhere, in all of human history, and throughout all eternity.

The Creator Spirit

When the Bible describes the creation of human beings, an even more intimate word is used for God's activity than is used with other parts of creation: "Then the Lord God formed man of dust from the ground, and breathed into his nostrils the breath of life; and man became a living being" (Gen. 2:7). The word for *breath* is *neshamah,* a closely related synonym to *wind* or *spirit.* We have a picture of God bending down over the still form of the body that He had shaped out of the dust of the earth and, in a kind of mouth-to-mouth resuscitation, actually breathing His own life into him. This specific activity of God breathing into the nostrils of man is not said of any other creature. It is true that breathing animals are sometimes described in the Bible as living beings, using exactly the same language that is used of human beings. But it is never said that God breathed into their nostrils the breath of life, nor is it ever said that they are made "in the image of God." This special relationship to God is reserved for human beings alone, and it means that human beings will be held responsible for the way they relate to God in obedience or rebellion.

In a general way, then, the Spirit of God is active throughout the entire created order, animate and inanimate. But, in a very special way, God's breath or Spirit brings man into being and puts human beings in a relationship to God that no other creature has. God's Spirit empowers a human being to live but does not control him like a puppet. Men and women are free to use this precious gift of life to love God and their neighbor. When the Russian cosmonauts, in one of their early space flights, radioed back to earth that they had not found any God out there, the very breath with which they mocked Him was given to them by the Creator God. How awesome is the responsibility we have to use this God-given breath in a way that will honor Him and bless the lives of others.

The Sustaining Spirit

In a closely related idea, the Bible also teaches us that the same Holy Spirit who brings us into being sustains our lives at every moment. The same Creator God who gives us life and breath can take it away, and we die. In Genesis 6:3 we read: "Then the Lord said, 'My spirit shall not abide in man for ever, for he is flesh, but his days shall be a hundred and twenty years" Because the Authorized or King James Version translated this, "My spirit shall not always strive with man," many interpreters have understood this passage to mean that God's Spirit would not keep "striving" with man to convict him of sin and bring him to salvation. There would be a time when the stubborn sinner would "cross the line" and God would give him up to destruction. This is a teaching which finds strong support in the Bible, as we shall see, but something else is being said here. The context tells us that God was reminding man that his days were limited. Man does not live by his own strength. He is frail flesh, and he lives only as long as God's creative Spirit sustains him.

This sobering truth could transform the life of mankind if only it could sink into the center of human consciousness. Even Christians seem to think that by certain laws of nature, created by God, they have been given life and, barring accident, they are likely to have a number of years in which to live out their choices and make their decisions. But this word from the Lord is a solemn reminder that we cannot take a single day for granted. Each day is a gift from God. Each breathing moment of life is sustained by the Spirit of a loving God. How can we ever afford to be careless about the way we use this precious gift?

The Human Spirit

Because the Spirit of God is the invisible power that brings human beings into existence and sustains them, the same word *ruach* is often used in the Pentateuch for the invisible human spirit which interacts with the divine Spirit in every human life. The Bible does not confuse the two because the human spirit has a mind and will of its own. Without the divine Spirit there would not be a human spirit to make any choices at all, but the divine Spirit does not make the choices for the human spirit. Human beings can grieve the Holy Spirit of God, using the divine gift of life to disobey the God who gave them life.[3]

In Genesis 41:8 we read that when Pharaoh awoke from his disturbing dream, "his spirit was troubled." Here "spirit" is used to define that aspect of human nature which most directly relates us to God. The activity of God's Spirit brought the troubling dream to Pharaoh, but Pharaoh's spirit responded to God's Spirit. This interaction of divine Spirit and human spirit is not just at the physical level of sustaining life. It is also at the level of human will and decision. It is the most intimate expression of the "image of God" in us, the capacity to interact responsibly with the living God. In short, the human spirit is that aspect of human nature with which we relate most directly to God.

Spirit as Human Vitality

In the thrilling account of Joseph and his brothers in Egypt, their grieving father, Jacob, could hardly believe them when he learned that Joseph was still alive: "But when they told him all the words of Joseph, which he had said to them, and when he saw the wagons which Joseph had sent to carry him, the spirit of their father Jacob revived" (Gen. 45:27). Here the term "spirit" simply means human vitality, including emotion, feeling, and attitude. Even so it is further evidence that human vitality is ultimately dependent upon the sustaining power of God's Spirit. There would not be any human vitality apart from the power of God.

When God sent Moses to the people of Israel in slavery in Egypt with the promise of deliverance from their suffering, "they did not listen to Moses, because of their broken spirit and their cruel bondage" (Ex. 6:9). The human spirit depends upon hope; when hope is gone, the spirit is crushed or broken. In a world threatened with nuclear destruction, with pain and suffering headlining the news every day, we are reminded that the survival of the human spirit depends upon the promise of God! Pity those who have no hope.

Spirit as Personal Attitude

Sometimes the word *spirit* simply means the attitude which a person expresses in life relationships. A suspicious husband had a "spirit of jealousy" come upon him (Num. 5:14); God "harden[ed] the spirit" of Sihon the king of Heshbon who refused to let the wandering Israelites pass through his land (Deut. 2:30). In these cases the persons were clearly responsible for their attitudes, and God held them accountable. Consistently, throughout the Bible, spirit is the area of our responsible interaction with God.

God commended his servant, Caleb "because he has a different spirit and has followed me fully" (Num. 14:24). Instead of the attitude of distrust and disobedience which had characterized so many of the Israelites, Caleb had shown a "different spirit" of faithful obedience and trust. It was all the more remarkable because it ran counter to the attitude of his fellow Israelites all around him. Again we see great emphasis placed on the freedom and responsibility of the human spirit.

The Redeemer Spirit

We have seen that the Creator Spirit of God brings the human spirit into being and interacts with it at every level of life. The other primary activity of God's Spirit in the Pentateuch is the effort to deliver His people from sin and slavery and to bring them into fellowship with Himself.

When Moses was commanded to gather seventy elders to share the burden of leading the people out of slavery into the Promised Land, God said: "I will take some of the spirit which is upon you and put it upon them; and they shall bear the burden of the people with you, that you may not bear it yourself alone" (Num. 11:17). The spirit of Moses was not put upon the elders. It was the Spirit of God, which had already been placed upon Moses to empower him to lead the people of Israel out of Egypt and into the wilderness of Sinai where they formed the covenant with God.

The redeeming activity of the Spirit is closely related to His creative activity. In fact, it is like the other side of the same coin. By creation, the Spirit brought us to be living beings; by His redemptive activity, the Spirit brings us to the fulfillment of His purpose in our lives. Creation and redemption are so close together that Paul could even speak of redemption as a "new creation" (2 Cor. 5:17). The Great Creator becomes our Great Redeemer, fulfilling in the new creation His original purpose in the old creation.

The Spirit of Prophecy

Continuing God's redemptive activity, some of the Spirit that was upon Moses was put upon the seventy elders "and when the spirit rested upon them, they prophesied" (Num.

11:25). When Joshua worried that this might diminish the leadership of Moses, he received a sharp rebuke: "Are you jealous for my sake? Would that all the Lord's people were prophets, that the Lord would put his spirit upon them!" (Num. 11:29).

Even a reluctant prophet, Balaam, was moved to utter an oracle of blessing upon Israel when "the Spirit of God came upon him" (Num. 24:2). Since the prophetic word was used to carry out God's purpose of redemption, the "spirit of prophecy" should be seen as another aspect of the redeeming activity of the Spirit of God.

The Succession of the Spirit

One further activity of the Spirit is seen in the Pentateuch —the passing of the Spirit from a divinely called leader to his successor. The Lord commanded Moses to "take Joshua the son of Nun, a man in whom is the spirit, and lay your hand upon him" (Num. 27:18). Moses obeyed the Lord and "took Joshua and caused him to stand before Eleazar the priest and the whole congregation, and he laid his hands upon him, and commissioned him as the Lord directed" (vv. 22-23).

This laying on of hands was the beginning of a long biblical tradition that extends all the way through the New Testament to the present time, as persons are set apart for particular ministries by the "laying on of hands." In this first instance, the context makes clear that two very important things are accomplished by this act: The individual is given a very powerful personal confirmation that God has put His Spirit upon him to enable him to accomplish the task to which he has been called; the ceremony of the laying on of hands is witnessed by the congregation as a sign and confirmation of God's choice of His servant to minister in their midst. The Spirit was not actually conferred by this physical act. The Spirit was already in Joshua, the son of Nun (Num.

27:18). God had already selected him. God was not dependent upon a human ritual to convey His Spirit to His chosen
servant. The ritual of the laying on of hands was a sign to
the individual and to the congregation that God had already
placed His Spirit upon the chosen leader and that the leader
would carry out his mission not in his own strength but in
the power of God.[4]

Analysis and Summary

There is no way to exaggerate the importance of these first
books of the Bible in laying a foundation for the doctrine of
the Holy Spirit. Everything else that is said in the Bible about
the Spirit, all that is taught in our Christian doctrines, and
all that is experienced in our Christian lives rests upon this
foundation. It should certainly assist our continuing study if
we can pull together these basic teachings about the Spirit in
an orderly way.

First and foremost is the absolute identification of the
Spirit with God Himself. God is Spirit, and *Spirit* becomes
the primary word for the invisible and powerful activity of
God in the world. The Bible emphasizes the holiness or
otherness of God, what theologians call His transcendence.
The counterbalancing emphasis upon the nearness and presence of God in the world and in our lives is what theologians
call God's immanence, His abiding in us and with us. This
is the role of the Holy Spirit, the indwelling presence and
power of God. The Spirit is not simply one aspect of God's
being or nature. The Spirit is God Himself, powerful and
present in His creation and in our lives.

The second important truth that is unfolded in the opening
pages of God's Word is that the Spirit of God is active in two
primary ways: in creation and in redemption.

In creation the Spirit is active in bringing everything into
existence and sustaining all things at every moment. In a very

special way, the Spirit or breath of God brings man and woman into existence and holds them accountable for the way they respond to the activity of God in their lives. This is the essential meaning of the "image of God" in us, our capacity and responsibility to relate to the Spirit of God as He works with our human spirits to accomplish His purpose in us.

The second primary way in which the Spirit of God works in human life and history is for our redemption, the bringing of men and women into a vital, personal relationship to God. This can be seen in the calling of special leaders (like Moses) to guide us in this journey with God or in the sending of the word of prophecy to instruct us along the way. Because this redemptive process continues as long as history unfolds, God has demonstrated His power to call new leaders in each generation and put His Spirit upon them.

The rest of the Bible is the story of how this creating and redeeming activity of God's Spirit continued with His people, from the wilderness to the Promised Land, in the times of the kingdom and the warnings of the prophets, in victory and in Exile, culminating in the ministry of Jesus and the outpouring of the Holy Spirit upon the church. For believers the Spirit is the clue to the whole Bible, the key that unlocks the meaning of human history.

Notes

1. This double meaning of *wind* and *spirit* presents translators with a problem. *The Good News Bible* translators have the "power of God" moving over the face of the waters rather than the "Spirit of God" (Gen. 1:2). God's invisible power was at work in the creation. To the Hebrews, God is personal; the "wind of God" is

as personal as His breath or His Spirit. See I. C. Heron, *The Holy Spirit* (Philadelphia: Westminster Press, 1983), pp. 3-10.

2. Paul even appealed to the Greek philosopher-poets Epimenides and Aratus in his famous sermon on Mars Hill: "In him we live and move and have our being" and "we are indeed his offspring" (Acts 17:28). This idea of the Universal Power permeating all of the cosmos was found even in Greek thought. It gave Paul a toe-hold in trying to preach the gospel to the Athenians.

3. Paul used this language in Ephesians 4:30: "Do not grieve the Holy Spirit of God, in whom you were sealed for the day of redemption." The power to please or grieve the Spirit of God is the distinctively human capacity, the image of God in us.

4. This is the root of the understanding of ordination to ministry that does not believe in "apostolic succession," the theory that the apostolic gift of ministry is transmitted by the laying on of hands in an unbroken succession from Simon Peter. Rather, God directly calls men and women for various ministries. Ordination is both a confirmation to the minister of his calling and the recognition by the congregation that they have seen the gifts of ministry in the life of the person whom they ordain.

2

The Holy Spirit in the Prophets

The second major division of the Hebrew canon of Scripture, our Old Testament, is called simply, the Prophets. This is exactly what Jesus called it when He named the three divisions of Scripture in a resurrection appearance to the disciples: "Everything written about me in the law of Moses and the prophets and the psalms must be fulfilled" (Luke 24:44).

This second division of the canon was further divided into the Former Prophets and the Latter Prophets. The Former Prophets consists of the books we usually call the Historical Books, through 2 Kings. The Latter Prophets consists of the great writing prophets, Isaiah, Jeremiah, and Ezekiel, together with the minor, or shorter, prophets through Malachi. Because these shorter writings are usually grouped in a single scroll about the length of the single scrolls of Isaiah or Ezekiel, they are simply called the Scroll of the Twelve.

The way in which this division of the canon of Scripture developed gives us a wonderful opportunity to follow the growth of the teaching about the Holy Spirit. We can see how the activity of the Holy Spirit was understood in the history of Judah and Israel, and we can compare that with the unique emphases in the writing prophets.

The Holy Spirit in the Historical Books

The one reference to "spirit" in the Book of Joshua is to the human spirit of the kings of the Amorites and the Canaanites who "heard that the Lord had dried up the waters of the Jordan for the people of Israel until they had crossed over, their heart melted, and there was no longer any spirit in them, because of the people of Israel" (Josh. 5:1). Their confidence or "spirit" was understandably broken when they saw the power of Israel's God.

But the "Spirit of the Lord" is a veritable refrain throughout the following book, the Book of Judges. In fact, the entire book is a story of the Spirit of God raising up one leader after another to deliver His people from invading armies. We would call them charismatic leaders today because they were called and filled by the Spirit of God to accomplish miracles that they could never have done in their own strength.

The Cycle of Sin and Deliverance

Judges follows the pattern laid out in chapter 3: "And the people of Israel did what was evil in the sight of the Lord, forgetting the Lord their God, and serving the Baals and the Asheroth" (Judg. 3:7). Their sin was followed by God's judgment: "Therefore the anger of the Lord was kindled against Israel, and he sold them into the hand of Cushanrishathaim king of Mesopotamia" (v. 8). Then would come their cry for deliverance: "But when the people of Israel cried to the Lord, the Lord raised up a deliverer for the people of Israel, who delivered them, Othniel the son of Kenaz, Caleb's younger brother" (v. 9).

In the case of Othniel, and many of the succeeding judges, it is simply said that "the Spirit of the Lord came upon him, and he judged Israel; he went out to war" (v. 10). The Spirit of God was the active power that was ruling and delivering

Israel, even though He used many human instruments: "But the Spirit of the Lord took possession of Gideon" (6:34); "Then the Spirit of the Lord came upon Jephthah" (11:29); and the entire life of Samson is told with the repeated refrain, "And the Spirit of the Lord began to stir him" (13:25); or "the Spirit of the Lord came mightily upon him, and he tore the lion asunder as one tears a kid" (14:6); even when Samson's wife betrayed his riddle to the Philistines and he was boiling with anger, "the Spirit of the Lord came mightily upon him, and he went down to Ashkelon and killed thirty men of the town" (v. 19).

The sad story of Samson's abuse of his God-given strength brought him, bound and blinded, to the prison in Gaza, deserted by the Spirit of the Lord. Even his last prayer for the return of his strength to bring down the idol temple of Dagon and let him die with the Philistines is a solemn reminder that God's judgment falls upon those who fail to acknowledge their dependence upon His spiritual power and who fail to use it according to His will.

An Evil Spirit from the Lord

One of the most surprising statements to appear at this point in the biblical record is that "God sent an evil spirit between Abimelech and the men of Shechem" (9:23). This spirit is not called the Holy Spirit, and, in the context, it is clear that God allowed the bitterness and hatred between wicked men to result in the ultimate accomplishment of God's purpose. But, from this point on, the Scriptures often say that God sent an evil spirit upon Saul or a lying spirit upon one of the false prophets, and it raises a moral question for us. Two things should be said in reference to this question.

First, biblical writers attributed everything directly to God, without making any distinction between what He permitted and what He initiated. Since God was the ultimate power behind everything, they did not shrink from affirming that anything that happened was in the will of God by permission or by direction, for good or for evil.[1] This is why we read that God moved David to number the people of Israel against God's own explicit commandment because God's anger was kindled against Israel and He was going to bring the consequences of this deed in judgment upon their heads (2 Sam. 24:1 *ff.*). In 1 Chronicles 21:1, the writer said, "Satan stood up against Israel, and incited David to number Israel." To place the direct blame upon Satan may have been very important for the theology of the chronicler, but he knew very well that Satan could do nothing without God's permission. Even if Satan and the evil spirits were responsible for their own evil actions, the biblical writers believed that God set severe limits for their action and that they could never seize control from the hands of God. Ultimately, the power of God ruled over everything, including both good and evil spirits.

In the second place, the sending of an "evil spirit" is a way of describing God's moral law of sin and retribution. The evil spirit between Abimelech and the men of Shechem was a consequence of their wicked deeds, showing God's inevitable judgment upon sin. He has built His moral law into the very fabric of the universe, and it is as dependable as the law of gravity. The "evil spirit" was the consequence of the violation of God's moral law; it came from God because, by His holy nature, sin is always condemned.

From this biblical teaching we understand that not all spirits in the world are good. Some spiritual powers oppose God. This is the background for the later warning that we must test the spirits, whether they be of God (see 1 John 4:1).

The Spirit upon Saul and David

The Books of Samuel carry out the theme of Judges. The Spirit of God came upon a person in order that he might lead God's people. This is what happened when Samuel the prophet anointed Saul and told him that he would rule over Israel (1 Sam. 10:1 *ff.*). The Spirit came mightily upon Saul, and he joined the band of prophets and prophesied with them (vv. 6,10). As long as Saul obeyed God, His Spirit was upon Saul.

Because of Saul's disobedience, the Lord rejected him (1 Sam. 16:1) and sent Samuel to find the shepherd boy David and anoint him to be king over Israel: "Then Samuel took the horn of oil, and anointed him in the midst of his brothers; and the Spirit of the Lord came mightily upon David from that day forward" (v. 13). As the laying on of hands was a sign of the bestowal of the Spirit, so the anointing with oil became a special sign of the coming of God's Spirit.

A remarkable thing happens in the very next verse: "Now the Spirit of the Lord departed from Saul, and an evil spirit from the Lord tormented him" (v. 14). It seems that in the very act of coming upon the young David, the Spirit was departing from Saul. The power of the Spirit to rule over Israel was taken from Saul and given to David. The choosing of David meant the rejection of Saul.

But an even more surprising thing is said: when the Spirit of the Lord was taken away, an evil spirit *from* the Lord was sent to torment Saul. If a person is abandoned by the Spirit of God, he seems to be in danger of being taken over by an evil spirit. One will be directed by the Holy Spirit or an evil spirit; he will not be left empty.[2]

This "evil spirit" seems to have been a kind of moodiness or depression that swept over Saul. He knew he had failed God and forfeited his great promise as a leader of his people.

This was the working out of God's judgment, as we saw in the Book of Judges. When David played his harp for Saul, Saul's spirits would be lifted, and the evil spirit would depart from him (1 Sam. 16:16,23). But Saul was only dealing with his symptoms. He refused the permanent cure for the fundamental disobedience which had brought about God's rejection of him and the taking away of God's Spirit.

The Contagious Spirit

The rest of the days of Saul were tormented by this spirit of jealousy of David. He threw a spear at David when the evil spirit rushed upon him (1 Sam. 18:10-11), or he sent messengers to capture or kill him (19:20 *ff.*). One of the most pathetic accounts in the Bible is Saul's futile effort to snatch David from under the protection of the Spirit.

When Saul sent messengers to take David, "they saw the company of the prophets prophesying, and Samuel standing as head over them"; then "the Spirit of God came upon the messengers of Saul, and they also prophesied" (v. 20). Outraged that his messengers had been "taken in" by the Spirit, Saul sent messengers a second and third time, and they also fell under the spell of the Spirit and joined the band of the prophets. Saul must have been livid! In desperation, he went to do the job himself; Saul also fell under the power of the Spirit, prophesying, stripping off all his clothes, and lying naked all day and all night. How he must have hated the taunt with which he had to live the rest of his life: "Is Saul also among the prophets?" (v. 24).

This episode portrays the Spirit of God as a kind of field of energy, like a massive electromagnet. When one enters the "field," that person is in danger of being captured by it. This description of the Spirit of God as a powerful and invisible force is consistent with biblical teaching from the very beginning. Sometimes He can even have a compulsive effect, seizing someone before one knows it. The developing doctrine of the Spirit moves toward a more personal emphasis and takes on the characteristics revealed by Jesus in the New Testament. But it never loses completely this dimension of an awesome and even dangerous power, which is never to be taken lightly. Even in the New Testament, lying to the Holy Spirit could result in instantaneous death (Acts 5:3 *ff.*).

Inspiring the Word

In the "last words of David," an oracle given in 2 Samuel 23, we have an explicit reference to the inspiration of the Holy Spirit in the life of the prophet or biblical writer: "The Spirit of the Lord speaks by me, his word is upon my tongue" (v. 2). David was not speaking, but the Spirit spoke by him. "His word is upon my tongue" reminds us that the word of God was often spoken before it was written, and the Spirit of God was just as active in the oral word as in the written Word.

What is said here in such a simple and direct way becomes a great theme in Scripture and in Christian doctrine: the inspiration of the Word of God. "The God of Israel has spoken" (v. 3) is the clue to the whole doctrine of inspiration. It means that even though God used David ("speaks *by* me") and did not violate his human personality, God still spoke His word through David. This is the fundamental element in our whole understanding of inspiration: God used human beings, empowered by His Spirit, to bring His Word directly to us. When we truly hear this Word, we are not listening to men but to God!

The Spirit upon Elijah and Elisha

The final teaching about the Spirit in the Former Prophets is found in the cycle of stories about Elijah and Elisha.

Obadiah, the servant of Ahab, was afraid to tell the king that he had found the hated Elijah because "as soon as I have gone from you, the Spirit of the Lord will carry you whither I know not" (1 Kings 18:12). Here is that same mysterious Power that seemed to take the prophet of the Lord wherever the Spirit wanted him to be. Obadiah knew better than to attempt a contest with the Spirit, as Saul had done.

When Micaiah stood against the false prophets of Ahab and prophesied Ahab's death at Ramoth-gilead, he told of his vision of a "lying spirit" that God allowed to go into the false prophets to entice Ahab to his death (22:21-23). This "lying spirit," like the "evil spirit" mentioned before, was allowed to carry out the judgment which God had already pronounced upon the wicked Ahab.

Elisha prayed for a "double portion" of Elijah's spirit as Elijah was about to be taken away into heaven (2 Kings 2:9, KJV). This recalls the sharing of Moses' spirit with the elders and with Joshua, but clearly God's Spirit was upon Moses and Elijah in the first place. The "sons of the prophets" at Jericho recognized that the spirit of Elijah had come upon Elisha, but they were afraid that the Spirit of the Lord might have taken Elijah "and cast him upon some mountain or into some valley" (v. 16). Against the protests of Elisha, they sent a band of men to search for him. This is another example of the belief that the Spirit is a strange, mysterious force which might do some violent and unpredictable things.

A characteristic of these historical books is that the Spirit of God is seen as the dynamic power by which God was moving in their lives and history, sometimes in judgment and sometimes in deliverance. We turn now to the writing prophets, in whom the *redemptive* activity of the Spirit is emphasized.

The Spirit in the Writing Prophets

Isaiah and Ezekiel were the great prophets of the Spirit. The other prophetic books have only limited references to the Spirit. Isaiah and Ezekiel do more to advance our understanding of the Holy Spirit than any other Old Testament writings. The New Testament teachings would be impossible to understand without them, and our Christian doctrine of the Holy Spirit is enriched by the contribution of these prophetic writings.

The Spirit in Isaiah

A new and important role of the Spirit is proclaimed in Isaiah: the anointing of the Messiah. The Hebrew word for *Messiah* means "anointed," and the context makes clear that the Messiah was to be anointed with the Spirit of God.

The first great passage on this anointing is found in Isaiah 11:1-3:

> There shall come forth a shoot from
>   the stump of Jesse,
>   and a branch shall grow out of
>   his roots.
> and the Spirit of the Lord shall
>   rest upon him,
>   and the spirit of wisdom and under-
>   standing,
>   the spirit of counsel and might,
>   the spirit of knowledge and the
>   fear of the Lord.
> And his delight shall be in the fear
>   of the Lord.

This beautiful passage tells us that the Anointed of the Lord will come out of the line of Jesse, the father of David, and enumerates the special gifts of the Spirit which will enable Him to fulfill His messianic mission.

A related passage in Isaiah 61:1-2, enumerates the things which the Anointed One will do on His mission:

> The Spirit of the Lord God is upon me,
>   because the Lord has anointed me
> to bring good tidings to the afflicted;
>   he has sent me to bind up the broken-
>   hearted,
> to proclaim liberty to the captives,
>   and the opening of the prison
>   to those who are bound;
> to proclaim the year of the Lord's
>   favor,
>   and the day of vengeance of our God;
> to comfort all who mourn.

Jesus read this passage in the synagogue in Nazareth, as a kind of inauguration of His mission, stopping at exactly this point in the text and infuriating His hometown hearers by His message (Luke 4:16-30). Evidently Jesus saw in this text from Isaiah the program of His ministry, and He fulfilled it to the letter. This close relationship between the Spirit and the ministry of the Messiah prepared the way for the later teaching about Father, Son, and Spirit.

As we have seen, the judgment of God upon people and nations is described in spiritual terms. In the judgment upon the princes of Egypt, "The Lord has mingled within her a spirit of confusion; and they have made Egypt stagger in all her doings" (Isa. 19:14). Even God's own people were punished with "a spirit of a deep sleep" closing their "eyes, the prophets" and covering their "heads, the seers" (29:10). This theme of the inexorable working out of God's judgment through His spiritual activity has become a familiar one in the Scriptures.

The activity of God's Spirit in healing and delivering His people is another theme of Isaiah. Although God's punishment fell upon His people, it continued only "until the Spirit is poured upon us from on high, and the wilderness becomes a fruitful field" (Isa. 32:15). Even though the people were scattered, "the mouth of the Lord has commanded, and his Spirit has gathered them" (34:16). This is another example of the close relationship between the Spirit and the word which comes from the mouth of the Lord. It is based upon the analogy of the breath which carries the spoken word. God's Spirit (or breath) carries His Word and enables it to accomplish His purpose.

The continuing creative activity of the Spirit, revealed in the opening chapters of the Bible, is echoed again in Isaiah. God created the heavens and the earth and "gives breath to the people upon it and spirit to those who walk in it" (42:5). But the weakness and dependence of the human spirit is emphasized by comparing the vaunted power of Egypt to the power of God: "The Egyptians are men, and not God; and their horses are flesh, and not spirit" (31:3). God proclaimed His continuing creative activity: "for from me proceeds the spirit, and I have made the breath of life" (57:16).

Isaiah called the rebellion of the people "griev[ing] his holy Spirit," but also recorded their yearning cry, "Where is he who put in the midst of them his holy Spirit" and reminded them that "like cattle that go down into the valley, the Spirit of the Lord gave them rest" (63:10-11,14). God would pour His Spirit upon their descendants and His blessing on their offspring (44:3).

A last theme of the Spirit is unique to Isaiah. The Suffering Servant of the Lord, who will bear the sins of the many, appears for the first time in Isaiah. In the teaching of Jesus and the early church, this Servant of the Lord was identified with Jesus the Messiah. This identification was made by Jesus Himself. In Isaiah, the Servant is first the nation of Israel (44:1; 49:3), a remnant of the people of Israel (49:6), and finally a mysterious figure who is "despised and rejected" and bears "the iniquity of us all" (53:3,6). No wonder the early Christians saw every detail of this sacrificial death of the Servant of the Lord fulfilled in Jesus.

The very first reference to the Servant includes the role of the Spirit:

> Behold my servant, whom I uphold,
>   my chosen, in whom my soul delights;
> I have put my Spirit upon him,
>   he will bring forth justice to the
>   nations.

Isaiah gave us a rich mine of teaching about the Spirit. From the creative activity of God's Spirit, to His judging and redeeming of His people, and culminating in the anointing of the Messiah/Servant of the Lord, Isaiah was truly a prophet of the Spirit.

The Spirit in Ezekiel

There are twenty-five references to the Spirit in the prophecy of Ezekiel. Most of these simply describe the Spirit taking up the prophet and moving him where God wanted him to go: "When he spoke to me, the Spirit entered into me and set me upon my feet" (Ezek. 2:2); "the Spirit lifted me up and took me away," and the prophet was carried to the exiles in Babylon by the river Chebar, where he "sat there overwhelmed among them seven days" (3:14-15). On another occasion, the Spirit lifted him up between heaven and earth and brought him "in visions of God to Jerusalem"

(8:3). The Spirit was Ezekiel's regular method of mobility, and he sometimes said explicitly that it is in a vision.

In Ezekiel's vision of the living creatures and the wheels, the Spirit seemed to drive them wherever they would go, and Ezekiel even said that "the spirit of the living creatures was in the wheels" (1:12,20-21). The Spirit was the energizing power which drove the wheels. The Spirit of God is the power which energizes all "living creatures." True to other biblical teaching, the invisible power of the Spirit is the dynamic energy by which God moved the prophet or disclosed His message in a vision or gave him the word to deliver to the people.

Ezekiel was the first to describe the redemption of God's people in terms of "a new spirit" within them. Although they were scattered in the Exile, far from home, God promised to gather them out of the foreign lands and bring them again to the land of Israel: "I will give them one heart, and put a new spirit within them; I will take the stony heart out of their flesh and give them a heart of flesh" (11:17,19). That is part of the background for the later New Testament teaching of regeneration by the Holy Spirit, bringing a new heart and a new life. This "new heart" and "new spirit" are promised again in Ezekiel 36:26-27. But the most powerful vision of all is the valley of dry bones, where the breath (or Spirit) of God sweeps over the bleaching bones and they rise up as "an exceedingly great host" (37:1-10). In the same way, God promised that those bones that "are the whole house of Israel" shall live again: "I will put my Spirit within you, and you shall live, and I will place you in your own land" (vv. 11-14). That is a great promise of resurrection and new life by the Spirit.

The message of Ezekiel is summarized in this ringing promise of the Lord: "I will not hide my face any more from them, when I pour out my Spirit upon the house of Israel"

(39:29). Ezekiel was the prophet of the new covenant, the new heart, and the new spirit in God's people by the power of the Spirit of the Lord.

The Spirit in the Other Prophets

Daniel and Hosea have few references to the spirit, and they are not references to the Spirit of God. But in Joel we have the classic passage which Peter quoted on the Day of Pentecost, a prophecy of the endtime, when God would pour out His Spirit upon all flesh:

> It shall come to pass afterward,
>   that I will pour out my spirit
>   on all flesh;
> your sons and your daughters
>   shall prophesy,
>   your old men shall dream dreams,
>   and your young men shall see
>   visions.
> Even upon the menservants and the
>   maidservants
>   in those days, I will pour out
>   my spirit (2:28-29).

This is one of the most glorious promises in all of Scripture, and it is noteworthy that God's Spirit will overcome the distinctions and segregation that have so plagued human life. Shocking as it must have seemed to Joel's contemporaries, God promised to pour out His Spirit on the daughters as well as the sons. And the prejudice that discriminates on the basis of age would be overcome: Both old and young will be given dreams and visions by the Spirit. In an outpouring of the Spirit that is down-right revolutionary, even the servants (or slaves), both male and female, would be included. This great prophecy is the forerunner of the vision of Paul that in Christ there will be no "Jew nor Greek, bond nor free . . . male or female," (Gal. 3:28, KJV).

Micah asked the rhetorical question, "Is the Spirit of the Lord impatient?" (Mic. 2:7), implying a negative answer; he insisted that, while the false prophets simply spoke to please the ones who fed them, his own word was true because he was "filled with . . . the Spirit of the Lord, and with justice and might" (Mic. 3:8). The prophet was inspired to emphasize the moral character of the Spirit of God, distinguishing Him from the spirit of the false prophets.

Haggai encouraged the people in the rebuilding of the Temple, despite its humble appearance, by reminding them of God's promise when they came out of Egypt: "My Spirit abides among you; fear not" (Hag. 2:5). The Spirit was simply God's presence in their midst; He had not forsaken them.

Zechariah reminded the people of their utter dependence upon God by his great text: "Not by might, nor by power, but by my Spirit, says the Lord of hosts" (Zech. 4:6). Only in the power of God's Spirit can we do anything that is truly good. He also reminded his hearers that the words of the Lord were "sent by his Spirit through the former prophets" (7:12). But he warned of a day when, because the prophets had spoken lies in the name of the Lord, those prophets and their "unclean spirit" would be taken away. Again, the evil or "unclean" spirit is designated as the power behind the false prophets. This is the background for the conflict between Jesus and the "unclean spirits" in the Gospels. The prophetic canon closes with a final reference to the creative "spirit of life," the power by which the Creator sustains and perpetuates the human race (Mal. 2:15).

Analysis and Summary

In this longest section of the Old Testament canon of

Scripture, our understanding of the person and activity of the Spirit of God has been advanced along several lines.

In the ongoing history of Israel, the prophets saw the Spirit of God not only raising up leaders to guide His people but also coming in judgment upon their sin and rebellion. The clue to the whole meaning and purpose of their history is that God is the energizing power. Behind all their victories and failures, their blessings and their punishment, was the powerful Spirit of God, working to accomplish His ultimate purpose of the redemption of His people.

The writing prophets sharpened this understanding of the Spirit. With the promise of a coming Messiah, anointed with the Spirit of the Lord, the redemptive purpose of God came to a new focus. The Messiah would bring a new day, when the Spirit would be poured out upon both men and women, slave and free, young and old. The Servant of the Lord, anointed with the Spirit, would give His life as a ransom for many. In the new day of redemption, God would put a new heart and a new spirit in them. The same Holy Spirit who was active in the original creation would bring about a new creation, fulfilling the purpose of God. Each of these elements is included in a complete formulation of the doctrine of the Holy Spirit.[3]

Notes

1. A beautiful exposition of the will of God as intentional, permissive, and circumstantial is found in a little book by Leslie D. Weatherhead, *The Will of God* (Nashville: Abingdon Press, 1944, 1972), 64 pp. It has brought comfort and understanding to countless people who have struggled to accept the tragedies of life. His

treatment of the "circumstantial will," pages 22 and following, develops the theme which we have mentioned here.

2. Jesus Himself taught us that a man may be cleansed of an evil spirit, only to have that spirit come back with "seven other spirits more evil than himself" (Luke 11:24-26). Nature abhors a vacuum, and human nature will be filled with some kind of spirit, good or evil.

3. Each of these biblical emphases enters into the development of a full doctrine of the Holy Spirit in Christian theology. One of the best illustrations of this process in found in George S. Hendry, *The Holy Spirit in Christian Theology* (Philadelphia: The Westminster Press, 1956), 128 pp. Each of the five chapters is devoted to an exposition of one of these biblical elements in the doctrine of the Spirit.

3

The Holy Spirit in the Writings

The last division of the Old Testament canon was originally the Psalms, the hymnbook of Israel. The Wisdom Literature, the historical Books of Chronicles, and the prophecy of Daniel were added before the rabbis closed the canon, near the end of the first century AD. Because the Psalms are concentrated on worship and personal devotion, a whole new dimension of the activity of God's Spirit is disclosed: the role of the Spirit in the personal life and worship of the believer. The other writings echo the same themes we have found in the earlier portions of the Old Testament.

The Holy Spirit in the Psalms

Even in the dire extremity of suffering, the faithful worshiper cries out, "Into thy hand I commit my spirit" (Ps. 31:5). This is Scripture from the Psalms that spoke so deeply to the need of the dying Jesus that it was His last word from the cross. Earlier He had cried out in the words of Psalm 22:1, "My God, my God, why hast thou forsaken me?"

The most persistent use of the word *spirit* in the Psalms designates the inner life of the worshiper. The spirit is that aspect of human personality that is most closely related to God. God blesses the one "in whose spirit there is no deceit" (32:2) and "saves the crushed in spirit" (34:18). The truly acceptable sacrifice to God is "a broken spirit" (51:17).

44

While crying out to God in the day of trouble, the psalmist meditated and his "spirit faints" (77:3). But "when my spirit is faint, thou knowest my way!" (142:3). This fainting spirit, also seen in Psalm 143:4 and 7, was lifted up by looking to God: "Let thy good spirit lead me on a level path" (v. 10). For the psalmist, the Spirit was not simply a doctrine; He was the intimate presence of God, without which the psalmist could not live a single day!

In one of the classic passages in all of Scripture, David confessed his terrible sin and cried out: "Create in me a clean heart, O God, and put a new and right spirit within me" (51:10). As we saw in Ezekiel, complete cleansing from sin requires a new heart and a new spirit, and only God can give it. It is a miracle of God's grace, and it is our deepest need. The next line, "Cast me not away from thy presence, and take not thy holy Spirit from me" (v. 11), reminds us that the awful consequence of sin is separation from God. The intimate relationship for which God made us is broken by sin. We can even see this in human relationships. When we sin against people and hurt them, the relationships are marred or broken. Only a genuine forgiveness can open the possibility of a renewed relationship.

In the great creation Psalm (104), the sustaining power of God's Spirit, revealed in the opening chapters of Genesis, is celebrated in some of the most beautiful words in the Bible. In a majestic panorama of the heavens and the earth, the psalmist sang of all the living things in God's creation: "When thou hidest thy face, they are dismayed; when thou takest away their breath, they die and return to their dust" (v. 29). What a poignant reminder that everything in this marvelous universe depends upon God at every moment! And God's creative work is not finished: "When thou sendest forth thy Spirit, they are created; and thou renewest the face of the ground" (v. 30). This renewing of the creation makes

possible the later New Testament vision of a "new heaven
and a new earth" which God will bring at the end of time.[1]

The last great emphasis of the psalmist was upon the
omnipresence of the Spirit, literally filling the whole universe. Nowhere can one escape His presence:

> Whither shall I go from thy Spirit?
>   Or whither shall I flee from thy presence?
> If I ascend to heaven, thou art there!
>   If I make my bed in Sheol, thou art there!
> If I take the wings of the morning
>   and dwell in the uttermost parts of the sea,
> even there thy hand shall lead me,
>   and thy right hand shall hold me (139:7-10).

The pervasiveness of God's Spirit is overwhelming. It might
be troubling to the sinner who is trying to hide something
from God because there is no way to escape Him. But, to the
psalmist, it was the most powerful message of comfort and
assurance. No matter what came, in life or in death, God
would be with him. In the first verse of this beautiful passage,
the two lines of Hebrew poetry parallel "thy Spirit" and "thy
presence." It provides one of the simplest and clearest definitions of God's Spirit in all of Scripture: God's Spirit is, quite
simply and profoundly, God's presence. There is no better
way to think of the Spirit of God than to remember that the
Spirit is God's presence with us, in joy or sorrow, in victory
or defeat, in life or in death.

The Spirit in Job

Because the Book of Job is dominated by the struggle of
that suffering man to understand what was happening to him
and why God seemed to be sending such punishment upon
him, the word *spirit* is used primarily for Job's spirit. He was
looking inward and agonizing over his own condition. But

through this devastating suffering, Job's faith persevered. He was confident of the Spirit and power of God, even in his deepest despair. These references to the Holy Spirit enrich the biblical teaching on this doctrine.

Those who "plow iniquity" perish by the "breath of God" and by "the blast of his anger" (4:8-9). The same divine power which brought the creation into being can come in judgment to destroy it. Eliphaz continued his discourse on the justice of God by describing "a spirit" which glided past his face, causing the hair of his flesh to stand up, and, out of the terrifying silence, asking the disturbing question: "Can mortal man be righteous before God?" (vv. 15-17). This visionary spirit does not seem to have been the Holy Spirit, but one of the spirits who serves God. It adds to the general biblical teaching that there are ministering spirits who serve God, sometimes identified as angels, but, at other times, simply called "spirits" or "ministering spirits."[2]

The Creator Spirit is seen again in Job: "By his wind [spirit] the heavens were made fair" (26:13); Job's own breath is sustained by God's Spirit: "As long as my breath is in me, and the spirit of God is in my nostrils; my lips will not speak falsehood, and my tongue will not utter deceit" (27:3-4). Even the "spirit in a man" which gives him understanding is called "the breath of the Almighty" (32:8). This implies more than physical breath or mental acumen. The "breath of God" gives us understanding that we could never attain in our human resources alone. Job found great reassurance, through all his suffering, in the conviction expressed by Elihu: "The spirit of God has made me, and the breath of the Almighty gives me life" (33:4). If God "should take back his spirit to himself, and gather to himself his breath, all flesh would perish together, and man would return to dust" (34:14-15). This perception of the Spirit of God permeating our physical lives gives a sacredness to human life and physical relationships, which we often ignore. We cannot divide our lives neatly into the physical and the spiritual, denigrating the physical and exalting the spiritual. Even the physical is permeated and sustained by the Spirit of God. The Book of Job continues some of the main teachings about the Spirit, but it emphasizes the power of God's Spirit to preserve his servant through devastating suffering.

The Spirit in Proverbs

Another of the Wisdom books, along with Job and the Psalms, is Proverbs. Like all the Wisdom Literature, it gives guidance for daily living in accord with the law of God. This was the meaning of *wisdom* in the Old Testament: practical instructions for living one's life in obedience to God. It had little to do with abstract knowledge; it was concerned with the urgent question of living in right relationship to God and neighbor.

This means that most references to the spirit in Proverbs are concerned with the human spirit of the faithful person. We are given a range of descriptions of the human spirit that runs the gamut of human emotions: the faithful spirit, the hasty spirit, the broken spirit, the haughty spirit, the humble spirit, the wounded spirit. God "weighs the spirit," even though man may be "pure in his own eyes" (16:2).

The remaining references to the Spirit in the last division of the Old Testament canon of Scripture echo the themes we have already seen. The Spirit of God came upon Azariah (2 Chron. 15:1) or upon Zechariah (2 Chron. 24:20) to accomplish His purpose through them. Surprisingly, God stirred up pagan kings to do His bidding (Pul, king of Assyria, 1 Chron. 5:26; 2 Chron. 36:22). God did not put His Spirit on them; rather, He stirred up their spirit. This makes them responsible for their spirit, and yet it provides a way for the prophetic writer to see the hand of God in the judgment which fell upon sinful Israel through the armies of their enemies. God can use the spirit that is obedient to Him; He can also work through or in spite of the spirit that rejects Him.[3]

Analysis and Summary

In the last division of the Old Testament, the Psalms give us the most insight into the nature and activity of God's Spirit. Only God can create a clean heart and put a new spirit in the sinner. Without the convicting, renewing power of the Spirit, there is no redemption and no hope for the guilty one.

The whole of creation is permeated by God's Spirit, making even the physical world the sphere of God's presence and God's grace. God is concerned about the physical needs, as well as the spiritual needs, of mankind. His spiritual activity in the old creation is the ground and assurance of the coming "new creation."

Nowhere in the whole universe, in life or in death, can we get away from God's presence, the Holy Spirit. This is the basis of the biblical teaching that even beyond death everyone must face God in the judgment. There is no escaping His omnipresent Spirit. But this same truth brings the glad assurance of eternal fellowship with God for those who have opened their lives to the regenerating power of His Spirit.

Although many people seem to think that the Holy Spirit only appeared on the earthly scene at Pentecost, we have seen that there is a rich and diverse background of the activity of the Spirit throughout the Old Testament. It is now possible to understand in a fuller way how the New Testament teaching about the Holy Spirit builds upon that foundation.

Notes

1. This vision of the "new heaven and new earth" is found in Revelation 21—22. It is the culmination of the creative work of God's Spirit which began in the first chapter of Genesis.

2. In Hebrews 1:14, these "ministering spirits" are "sent forth to serve, for the sake of those who are to obtain salvation."

3. Leslie Weatherhead, *The Will of God* (Nashville: Abingdon Press, 1944, 1972) is especially helpful in understanding how God can work through both good and evil circumstances to accomplish His holy purpose. See especially pp. 24 *ff.*

4

Jesus and the Spirit

Upon this broad foundation of Old Testament teaching concerning the Spirit of God, which we have surveyed in the preceding chapters, the Gospel writers set forth the climactic revelation of the Spirit in the person and ministry of Jesus. From the Christian perspective, Jesus is the supreme revelation of God in human history. This includes the supreme revelation of God as Spirit in the life of Jesus. To this teaching about the Holy Spirit in the life and ministry of Jesus, we now turn.

The Birth of Jesus

The accounts of the birth of Jesus in the Gospels fittingly emphasize the activity of God in the totality of His Being as Father, Son, and Holy Spirit. The Son of God, and the Son of God only, "was made flesh" through Mary. The Bible makes that abundantly clear. There is never any confusion on this point.

For this reason, it is most unfortunate that the phrase "mother of God" came to be applied to Mary in the early centuries of church debate about the person of Jesus.[1] In that debate, the phrase "mother of God" simply meant that Jesus was already the divine Son of God when he was begotten in the womb of Mary; therefore, she gave birth to a baby who was the Son of God in human flesh when He was born. He did not become the Son of God later by adoption, as some heretical theologians argued, either at His baptism or His resurrection. That Jesus was divine from the very moment of conception is clearly taught in the Gospels. Because the word *God* usually signifies the Father-Creator, the phrase "mother of God" sounds as if Mary is the source of Deity. To the naive mind, it may suggest that God came into Being through Mary. God's Son came into human flesh through Mary, but His Being is eternal. Otherwise, He could not be God.

Luke spelled this out in clear and beautiful language: "Gabriel was sent from God to a city of Galilee named Nazareth, to a virgin betrothed to a man whose name was Joseph, of the house of David; and the virgin's name was Mary" (Luke 1:26-27). When Gabriel told Mary that she would conceive in her womb "and bear a son" and should "call his name Jesus," Gabriel said explicitly that this child would "be called the Son of the Most High" (vv. 31-32). In astonishment Mary asked how this could happen and received the answer that has been orthodox Christian theology for twenty centuries:

> The Holy Spirit will come upon you,
> and the power of the Most High
>   will overshadow you;
> therefore the child to be born
>   will be called holy,
> the Son of God (v.35).

It would be difficult to imagine how this great doctrine of the incarnation of the Son of God could be expressed in more chaste and simple language. No suggestion is found here of sexual cohabitation between divine and human beings, as in Greek mythology. The "Most High" is certainly the Father-Creator. The "power of the Most High" is the Holy Spirit, revealed throughout the Bible as the invisible but powerful presence of God. The Child to be born would be called the Son of God. This is a functional view of the Trinitarian activity of God, long before Christian theologians had ever formulated a doctrine of the Holy Trinity in the fourth and fifth centuries.[2]

Matthew supported this statement about the activity of the Holy Spirit at the conception of Jesus in his independent account: "Now the birth of Jesus Christ took place in this way. When his mother Mary had been betrothed to Joseph, before they came together she was found to be with child of the Holy Spirit" (Matt. 1:18).

By saying "before they came together," Matthew excluded the possibility that Joseph could be the biological father of Jesus. In the phrase "of the Holy Spirit," Matthew used the Greek preposition *ek,* meaning "out of." The Holy Spirit was the source of Mary's "child," not Joseph. This is the biblical answer to the haunting question of the beautiful Christmas carol, "What Child Is This?"

When the angel appeared to Joseph in a dream, urging him not to be afraid to take Mary as his wife, even more explicit language was used: "for that which is conceived in her is of the Holy Spirit" (v. 20). Here the biological event of conception is attributed to the activity of the Holy Spirit. This is the real meaning of the doctrine of the virgin birth. It has nothing to do with the theory of the "perpetual virginity of Mary," which developed later in church history. On the contrary, Matthew made clear that Mary and Joseph had four sons, who are named, and a plural number of daughters, who are not named (13:55-56). In this event of the incarnation of the Son of God, the Divine Power bypassed the procreative process that He had ordained in the creation. He begot Jesus directly, thereby making a new beginning in the human race. This is why Jesus can be called a "new Adam." God began the human race again in Jesus.

Mary's Visit to Elizabeth

Immediately after the announcement to Mary that she would bear the Son of God, she "went with haste" to visit her relative, Elizabeth, who was about to become the mother of John the Baptist. Although Elizabeth's conception was certainly a miracle, considering her extreme age and that of her husband, there was never any suggestion that John the Baptist was conceived by the Holy Spirit. In fact, the words of Scripture make it abundantly clear that Zechariah was the father, even as Elizabeth was the mother, in the announcement of the angel: "Your wife Elizabeth will bear you a son, and you shall call his name John" (Luke 1:13).

But something *is* said about the activity of the Holy Spirit in the life of Elizabeth. She was inspired to give a beautiful blessing to the young virgin who would become the mother of her Lord: "And when Elizabeth heard the greeting of Mary, the babe leaped in her womb; and Elizabeth was filled with the Holy Spirit and she exclaimed with a loud cry, Blessed are you among women, and blessed is the fruit of your womb!' " (Luke 1:41-42).

The significance of this experience for Mary, and for the later Christian community which treasured these words, was that the Holy Spirit, through Elizabeth, confirmed Gabriel's promise to Mary. Mary was not left to wonder if something were wrong with her mind, or if she were having hallucinations. After all, her experience was without parallel in all of human history. How could she be sure? The same Holy Spirit who overshadowed Mary bore witness through Elizabeth that, indeed, Mary was to be the mother of the Lord. How much Mary needed this reassurance! And the Holy Spirit was going to bear further witness to the holy Child of Mary.

The Witness of Simeon

It may be very significant that there is no reference to the Holy Spirit in the beautiful account of the actual birth of Jesus. There were heavenly visitors, to be sure; they brought the glorious good news of the birth of the Savior. But the birth of the Babe was painfully earthy, with no room in the inn and only the crude surroundings of a stable to shelter that blessed event. Perhaps that is the Bible's way of reminding us how utterly and fully human was this Baby who was, and is, at the same time, the eternal Son of God.

But the Holy Spirit came to center stage with the presentation of Baby Jesus in the Temple. A powerful and public witness was borne to Jesus as the promised Messiah by the activity of the Holy Spirit in a devout old man named Simeon. No doubt many mothers in Israel had hoped that they might bear a son who would be the Messiah. And, as often happens, many parents and relatives expressed exaggerated hopes for a newborn child or grandchild. They always have. But the Scripture makes three exceptional statements about the Holy Spirit preparing Simeon to recognize and bless Baby Jesus: "Now there was a man in Jerusalem, whose name was Simeon, and this man was righteous and devout, looking for the consolation of Israel, and the Holy Spirit was upon him" (Luke 2:25). This first statement about the Spirit being upon Simeon alerts us to the fact that, although there might have been many righteous and devout people in Israel, the special power of the Holy Spirit was upon Simeon in such a way that his words and actions were from God Himself.

Then a second thing was said about the activity of the Spirit in the life of Simeon: "It had been revealed to him by the Holy Spirit that he should not see death before he had seen the Lord's Christ (v. 26). Now we can be sure that the "consolation of Israel," for which Simeon was looking in the

first reference, really meant that he was looking for the
Lord's Anointed, the promised Messiah, to deliver His people. We have the added word that the Holy Spirit had assured Simeon that he would see the Messiah before he died.
Not only did the Spirit confirm this marvelous event to Elizabeth when she met Mary but the same Holy Spirit had prepared the heart of Simeon beforehand to recognize the divine
Child when He came. In fact, all three tenses of the activity
of the Holy Spirit are revealed in these birth narratives: in
the past, Simeon had been prepared to expect the Messiah
before he died; in the present, the Holy Spirit overshadowed
Mary and the Messiah was conceived in her; then after that
conception, Elizabeth, filled with the Spirit, bore witness that
Mary was, indeed, to be the mother of the Messiah.

With all the people coming and going in the Temple, it
would have been very unlikely that old Simeon would have
happened to encounter just this couple and just this Baby
among the thousands. This brings us to the third and final
statement about the Spirit in the life of Simeon:

> And inspired by the Spirit he came into the temple; and when
> the parents brought in the child Jesus, to do for him accord-
> ing to the custom of the law, he took him up in his arms and
> blessed God and said,
>
> > "Lord, now lettest thou thy servant
> >   depart in peace,
> > according to thy word;
> > for mine eyes have seen thy
> >   salvation" (vv. 27-30).

With the Spirit upon his life, and with the Spirit revealing to
him beforehand that he would see the Messiah, the Holy
Spirit still had to lead the old man to the right place, at the
right time, to meet the child Jesus. The Wise Men were led
by a star to the Christ child. But Simeon was led by the Holy

Spirit to the Christ child. And so it is with us. None of us can find our way to Jesus until the Holy Spirit leads us.

The Witness of John the Baptist

The angel had said to Zechariah, the father of John the Baptist, that his child would "be filled with the Holy Spirit, even from his mother's womb" (Luke 1:15) and would go before the Lord "in the spirit and power of Elijah" (v. 17). Like many of the Old Testament leaders and prophets, John would be filled with the Spirit to carry out his appointed mission, preparing the way for the Messiah. It was never said or suggested that John was conceived by the Holy Spirit. Only Jesus was conceived by the Spirit. But, like many other divinely chosen leaders, John was filled with the Spirit to enable him to do something that in his human strength, he could never accomplish. When John was born and Zechariah's speech was restored, the happy father "was filled with the Holy Spirit and prophesied, saying, Blessed be the Lord God of Israel, for he has visited and redeemed his people" (vv. 67-68).

When John preached in the Jordan Valley, he proclaimed the Coming One "who is mightier than I, the thong of whose sandals I am not worthy to stoop down and untie" (Mark 1:7). Then John made another significant contrast: "I have baptized you with water; but he will baptize you with the Holy Spirit" (v. 8). This clearly identified Jesus as the Messiah because He was the One who was anointed with the Spirit; He was the only one who could baptize with the Holy Spirit. If there were any doubt that this promise pointed toward Pentecost, the parallel passages in Matthew 3:11 and Luke 3:16 remove it: "He will baptize you with the Holy Spirit and with fire." The tongues of flame that accompanied the rushing mighty wind at Pentecost (Acts 2:2-4) were the explicit fulfillment of this promise of the baptism with the Holy Spirit and fire.

Finally, this witness of John the Baptist is powerfully confirmed in the Gospel of John:

> John bore witness, "I saw the Spirit descend as a dove from heaven, and it remained on him. I myself did not know him; but he who sent me to baptize with water said to me, 'He on whom you see the Spirit descend and remain, this is he who baptizes with the Holy Spirit.' And I have seen and have borne witness that this is the Son of God" (John 1:32-34).

John recognized Jesus as the Messiah by the Spirit of God descending upon Him and remaining. Throughout the Old Testament revelation, the Spirit came and went, only temporarily abiding upon a judge like Samson, or a prophet like Ezekiel. But, upon Jesus, the Spirit came to abide. This marked Jesus as the Anointed One, the promised Messiah. The One who was anointed with the Spirit would baptize with the Spirit, John promised. The Spirit who anointed Jesus for His messianic mission would baptize His followers for their mission in the world.

The Baptism of Jesus

One of the most significant actions of the Holy Spirit in the entire Bible was His descent upon Jesus at His baptism. It was such an epochal experience for Jesus and assumed such importance in the apostolic witness to His messiahship that some Christian theologians even argued that Jesus became the Son of God at the moment when the Holy Spirit descended "like a dove" upon Him. Fortunately, the Bible makes it clear that Jesus was the Son of God from all eternity and was, therefore, divine when He was conceived and born as the Son of Mary. He did not have to wait until the baptism or resurrection or ascension to be "adopted" as the Son of God. On these biblical grounds, the church condemned this theory of "adoptionism" for the heresy that it was.[3]

What *did* happen at the baptism of Jesus was that the Holy Spirit descended upon Him to anoint Him for His messianic mission. Even though Jesus had been begotten by the Holy Spirit, it was necessary that the Holy Spirit designate and empower Him to fulfill the mission for which He had come into the world. The accounts of the baptism show plainly that the descent of the Holy Spirit was a powerful confirmation and appointment of Jesus as the Messiah. "And when he came up out of the water, immediately he saw the heavens opened and the Spirit descending upon him like a dove; and a voice came from heaven, 'Thou art my beloved Son; with thee I am well pleased.' " (Mark 1:10-11).

The heavenly voice spoke directly to Jesus: "*Thou* art my beloved Son"! Certainly Jesus needed this divine confirmation of His mission and the powerful anointing of the Spirit to accomplish it. The Gospel accounts do not make entirely clear exactly how much the crowds at the Jordan River saw, heard, or understood of this miraculous event. Luke used almost the same words as Mark, emphasizing that the heavenly voice spoke directly to Jesus: "Thou art my beloved Son; with thee I am well pleased" (Luke 3:22). Matthew had the voice speaking to the bystanders: "This is my beloved Son, with whom I am well pleased" (Matt. 3:17). This is another case of the multiple witness of the Gospels undergirding an important theological truth: The heavenly voice and the anointing by the Holy Spirit accomplished the double purpose of confirming to Jesus and bearing witness to the bystanders that He was, indeed, the long-awaited Messiah. At least one bystander, John the Baptist, had been given the divine revelation that he would recognize the Messiah by the descent of the Holy Spirit upon Him (John 1:29-34). It required the witness of the Holy Spirit then, and it requires the witness of the Holy Spirit now, to convince us that Jesus is, indeed, the Messiah, the Son of God.

The Temptation of Jesus

All of the Gospel writers emphasize that the Holy Spirit who came upon Jesus with power at His baptism never left Him throughout His entire ministry. Everything Jesus did was in the power of the Spirit. This was one of the grand marks which distinguished Jesus from all of the charismatic leaders of the Old Testament.

Yet, it is shocking to read that immediately after Jesus' baptism, the Spirit "drove him out into the wilderness" (Mark 1:12) to face the temptation by Satan. The powerful Spirit of God, who anointed Jesus for His messianic mission, was now driving Him to a confrontation with the evil one. Why would the Holy Spirit do such a thing? The answer to this question gives us a clue to the meaning of the mission of Jesus in this world.

The Bible tells us that the first man and woman, Adam and Eve, faced the tempter in the lush setting of the primeval garden of Eden (Gen. 3). Now the "last Adam," as Paul called Jesus (1 Cor. 15:45), faced the same tempter, after forty days of hunger and thirst in a barren desert. This was not a casual event in the narrative of the life of Jesus. It was absolutely crucial for His redemptive mission. Because the first Adam failed in his encounter with the tempter, it was imperative that the last Adam win the victory over the power of the evil one and start humankind on a new track.

Some people seem to think that if Jesus had accepted the suggestions of Satan He would somehow have ceased to be divine. But Jesus' divinity was not at stake in the wilderness temptation; our salvation was hanging in the balance! We know that, according to the Gospel record, Jesus had thought about His special relationship to God as His Father at twelve years of age in the Temple. Then the voice from heaven confirmed His divine Sonship at His baptism in the Jordan.

When Satan struck with his first temptation, he also acknowledged the divine Sonship of Jesus and tried to exploit that very power for his own purposes: "If you are the Son of God, command these stones to become loaves of bread" (Matt. 4:3). The grammatical form of the words "If you are" in the original Greek of Matthew's Gospel, requires that both the speaker and the one addressed assume the condition to be true: "*Since you are* the Son of God" is a literal and accurate rendering of the words.[4] Satan knew very well that Jesus was the Son of God. Precisely because of that fact, Satan tried to persuade Jesus to use His divine power in a way that would undermine the mission of Jesus to redeem the world. The Holy Spirit led Jesus to this encounter with Satan because without the victory over the Tempter Jesus could never have become the Savior of those who had fallen under Satan's power.

The Holy Spirit Will Speak Through the Disciples

In one of the promises which Christians have claimed down through the centuries, Jesus assured His disciples that when they were dragged into the synagogues, before "the rulers and the authorities," they should not be anxious how or what to answer because "the Holy Spirit will teach you in that very hour what you ought to say" (Luke 12:12). In Mark's account, the words are even more direct: "Do not be anxious beforehand what you are to say; but say whatever is given you in that hour, for it not you who speak, but the Holy Spirit" (Mark 13:11).

Apparently this is a promise of Jesus that was fulfilled only after the coming of the Spirit upon the disciples at Pentecost. We know that they were not dragged into the synagogues or before rulers and authorities until after the death, resurrection, and ascension of Jesus. We also know that the Holy Spirit came upon them with power to be witnesses to Jesus at Pentecost (Acts 1:8; 2:4,33). The same Holy Spirit who indwelt and impowered Jesus then indwelt and empowered His followers. The redemptive power of the Spirit of God, who worked through Jesus, continued to work redemptively through the lives of the apostles.

Casting Out Demons by the Spirit of God

When the Pharisees accused Jesus of casting out demons by Beelzebul, the prince of demons, Jesus came right back with an invincible argument: "If Satan casts out Satan, he is divided against himself; how then will his kingdom stand?" (Matt. 12:26). Jesus then drew the conclusion that left them self-condemned in their blasphemy: "But if it is by the Spirit of God that I cast out demons, then the kingdom of God has come upon you" (v. 28). If even the divine Son of God was empowered by the Holy Spirit to cast out demons, or work His other redemptive miracles, how much more must we depend utterly upon the power of the Spirit to accomplish God's purpose through our lives!

Blaspheming the Spirit

Now we are in a position to consider the age-old question of the unpardonable sin. In this very passage of Scripture, in which Jesus was casting out demons by the Spirit of God (Matt. 12:22-32; Mark 3:20-30; Luke 11:14-23), the Pharisees committed the unforgivable sin of blaspheming the Holy Spirit. They knew full well that only the Holy Spirit of God could be accomplishing these miracles they saw Jesus doing. They considered themselves the exclusive channel of God's working in the world. When they realized that the Spirit of God was bypassing them and working through an uneducated country prophet from Galilee, they decided to defy and blaspheme God Himself. How they hated Jesus and the Spirit of God who worked through Him! They were humiliated that, with all their religious knowledge and power, God had passed them by and was using this man whom they viewed with such contempt.

People have sometimes defended the Pharisees by saying, "Surely if these religious leaders had really understood that it was the Spirit of God working through Jesus, they would not have accused him of being in league with Satan." But that is exactly the point. It was precisely because the Pharisees knew perfectly well that only the Spirit of God could be working these miracles that they were able to commit this heinous sin against the Holy Spirit. It was a deliberate defiance of the power of God because the Spirit was not using the Pharisees and their religious rituals. Anyone who does not see the danger of using even our religious institutions in defiance of the will of God does not yet understand the nature of sin. Those who are very religious are in the greatest danger of committing this monstrous sin that Jesus condemned in such chilling words:

> Therefore I tell you, every sin and blasphemy will be forgiven men, but the blasphemy against the Spirit will not be forgiven. And whoever says a word against the Son of man will be forgiven; but whoever speaks against the Holy Spirit will not be forgiven, either in this age or in the age to come (Matt. 12:31-32).

Only by the Spirit of God can we recognize and believe in Jesus as the Son of God. If we reject and blaspheme the Holy Spirit, shutting Him out and driving Him away, no avenue remains by which God may bring us to salvation. This is why the sin against the Holy Spirit is unforgivable: He is the only

One who can draw us to the Son and to the Father. If we reject the Spirit, the door of forgiveness is forever closed.

Praying for the Spirit

Even a casual reading of the four Gospels will show that Luke had a special interest in prayer and in the Holy Spirit. Luke called attention to prayer-events in the life of Jesus which no other evangelist mentioned. Only Luke recorded the saying of Jesus about praying for the Holy Spirit: "If you then, who are evil, know how to give good gifts to your children, how much more will the heavenly Father give the Holy Spirit to those who ask him!" (Luke 11:13). In the parallel passage, Matthew said, "How much more will your Father who is in heaven give good things to those who ask him!" (Matt. 7:11). Of course, no "good thing" or "good gift" could be greater than the gift of the Holy Spirit. When we put these two passages together, we see that the greatest answer to our prayers may not be in the "good things" we are asking for, but in the gift of the Holy Spirit whom we need more than anything. God knows what gift we need far better than we know what to ask. This powerful promise of Jesus reminds us that the gift of the Holy Spirit comes in answer to our faithful prayer.

Jesus Breathes the Holy Spirit into the Disciples

In John's Gospel, special emphasis is given to the coming of the Holy Spirit into the lives of the believers after Jesus had been "glorified." A careful study of John reveals that Jesus was glorified by being "lifted up" on the cross. The "glory" of God is His innermost nature or being. The deepest nature of God is disclosed as sacrificial love by the death of Jesus on Calvary's cross.

On the "great day," or seventh day, of the Feast of Tabernacles, Jesus stood and proclaimed, "If any one thirst, let him come to me and drink. He who believes in me, as the scripture has said, 'Out of his heart shall flow rivers of living water' " (John 7:37-38). It was customary to carry a pitcher of water from the pool of Siloam each day of the feast, and Jesus probably spoke these words as the sacred water was poured out in a ritual offering in the Temple. But John did not leave us wondering about the meaning. In the very next sentence he made the spiritual significance abundantly clear: "Now this he said about the Spirit, which those who believed in him were to receive; for as yet the Spirit had not been given, because Jesus was not yet glorified" (v. 39).[5] John established a chronology of the coming of the Spirit. In fact, there is a mutually exclusive ministry of the Holy Spirit in the life of the historical Jesus, and then, later, in the lives of those "who believed in him." As long as Jesus was here in His earthly ministry, the Holy Spirit worked specifically through Him in His *redemptive* activity. After the death and resurrection of Jesus, the Holy Spirit was given to Jesus' disciples so that they might continue the same ministry which He had begun. If there were any doubt about this, John removed it by his graphic account of the appearance of Jesus to His disciples on the evening of the resurrection day: "Then the disciples were glad when they say the Lord. Jesus said to them again, 'Peace be with you. As the Father has sent me, even so I send you." And when he had said this, he breathed on them, and said to them, "Receive the Holy Spirit' " (John 20:20-22). Only ten of the disciples were present for this intimate gift of the "breath" of Jesus, the Holy Spirit, from the resurrected Lord to the band of disciples who would continue Christ's ministry. Thomas was absent; and Judas, the betrayer, was already dead. I think this intimate gift of the spiritual power of Jesus to His disciples was not, as many scholars say, a dual account by John of the Pentecost experience of Acts 2. I think it is a very significant separate event. It differs from Luke's account of the outpouring of the Holy Spirit at Pentecost in several important ways:

1. The Pentecost experience was very public, with a sensational display of rushing wind, tongues of fire, and animated proclamation of the good news of Jesus in the languages of the Mediterranean world. That is exactly the point: Pentecost was the launching of the worldwide mission of Jesus from Jerusalem, to Judea, to Samaria, and to the "uttermost parts" of the earth. The breathing of Jesus upon the disciples in John 20:22 is the very personal and very private gift of the life and power of the Spirit to them. As the Father sent forth Jesus in the power of the Spirit, so Jesus sent forth the disciples in the power of the Spirit. Just as Jesus had been begotten by the Holy Spirit at the beginning of His incarnational life, so the disciples were being "born of the Spirit" (see John 3:5) as they took up the ministry of Jesus and continued it in their lives.

2. The entire body of believers, including the women, were "all filled with the Holy Spirit" at Pentecost (Acts 2:4). This is exactly the theme of Luke in Acts, that the Holy Spirit included in His embracing power Jews and Greeks, men and women, slaves and free persons. John's emphasis was upon the power of the Spirit to generate new life; Luke's emphasis was upon the power of the Spirit to spread the gospel of Jesus Christ to the ends of the earth.

3. The most striking difference between the two accounts of the coming of the Holy Spirit in John 20 and in Acts 2 is that John described the bestowal of the Spirit *directly by Jesus,* as He breathed upon the disciples. There had been nothing like that in biblical history since the time that God breathed into the nostrils of man "the breath of life; and man became a living being" [soul]" (Gen. 2:7). This is the point: God, who generated new life made in His image in the old creation, was generating through Jesus, the Word made

flesh, a new kind of humanity made in the image of Christ. The Holy Spirit in Acts anointed the band of believers, 120 in number, only after Jesus had returned to the "right hand of God, and having received from the Father the promise of the Holy Spirit, he has poured out this which you see and hear" (Acts 2:33). The interrelationship of Father, Jesus, and the Holy Spirit, which Peter spelled out in his sermon at Pentecost, is matched by the Paraclete sayings in John's Gospel, which we shall examine in the next chapter.

Born of the Spirit

With this chronology of the Spirit dwelling first in Jesus, during His incarnate ministry, and then being breathed into the disciples by the risen Lord, we are now in a position to understand one of the most controversial sayings of Jesus about the Holy Spirit in the Gospel of John.[6] In the famous conversation with Nicodemus, a ruler of the Jews, Jesus said: "Truly, truly, I say to you, unless one is born of water and the Spirit, he cannot enter the kingdom of God" (John 3:5).

Some interpreters have argued that "born of water" must mean John's baptism since that is the only one mentioned to this point in John's Gospel and the only baptism Nicodemus could possibly know about. Others argue that "born of water" must mean Christian baptism, although it had not yet been given or commanded; some interpret this to be the means by which they are "born" into the kingdom of God. Still others argue that the phrase "born of water" refers to the physical birth since the fetus is surrounded by the fluid-filled placenta, which breaks during the birth process.

Each of these interpretations is pointing toward a significant Christian truth; but every one of them misses an important point that John was making all through his Gospel. As we have seen, the Spirit was not given until the resurrected Lord breathed the Holy Spirit into the disciples, generating a new life in them and "sending them forth" into the world, as the Father had sent Jesus. This parallel to the conception of Jesus by the Holy Spirit in the womb of the virgin Mary is important: the Johannine way of explaining the mission of Jesus is that the Father sent Him, empowered by the Spirit, to carry out that mission; now, the same Holy Spirit who empowered Jesus was generating new life in the disciples and sending them forth on their ministry in the world. But this birth by the Spirit cannot occur until the death and resurrection of Jesus, so the word to Nicodemus was a prophecy and a promise, fulfilled when "the Spirit is given."

Those who take "born of water" to mean John the Baptist's baptism are right at one point: John's baptism of repentance for the remission of sins was a sign of the messianic age and was a preview of the baptism of the Spirit which was to come through Jesus. But the baptism of the Spirit was precisely what John's baptism could not do! Only the One coming after John, the Messiah, could baptize with the Holy Spirit. John did not bestow the Spirit; Jesus did. John did not bring people into the kingdom; Jesus did. John's baptism was a prophetic sign, and John was the forerunner of the Messiah; but John did not baptize with the Spirit, and John was not the Messiah.

Those who think "born of water" means Christian baptism also have one valid point: that baptism was yet to come in the future, when Jesus completed His earthly mission and commanded His disciples to baptize in His name. However, as often interpreted, it attributes a magical power to the act of water baptism, as if that ritual, correctly performed, could somehow save. Such an interpretation misses the whole point of "spiritual birth," which Jesus was describing in this passage, and contradicts the entire teaching of the Bible. God is not locked into or limited by any religious ritual! He can save a dying thief on the cross without water baptism; He can send His Spirit upon a band of Gentiles while Peter was still preaching, before they even thought of "water for baptizing" (Acts 10:47). Christian baptism is the sign and confession of Jesus Christ as Lord, by the power of the Holy Spirit, who generates this new life in the believer. No ritual of water baptism, or any other religious rite, can limit or restrict the Spirit of God in saving "those who believe."

Those who believe that "born of water" in John 3:5 refers to the physical birth also have a point. There is no doubt that Jesus was contrasting the spiritual birth with the physical birth that Nicodemus had suggested. The very next verse makes this explicit: "That which is born of the flesh is flesh, and that which is born of the Spirit is spirit" (v.6). The spiritual birth was being contrasted with the physical birth; but the form of the Greek language requires that the "water" be joined with the word "Spirit," putting both "water" and "Spirit" on the side of the spiritual birth. Because the Greek does not repeat the article "the" with each word, they cannot be grammatically separated; they could even be joined with a hyphen, making a "water-Spirit" birth. That puts both of these words squarely in the middle of "new birth" or "birth from above," about which Jesus was speaking to Nicodemus. Water, Word, and Wind (Spirit) are all powerful signs of the cleansing, regenerating power of the Holy Spirit throughout John's Gospel; and water and Spirit combine here to describe the miracle of the new birth (see John 6:63; 15:3; 19:34).

Summary

As we should expect, everything we have learned about the Holy Spirit in the entire biblical history has come to brilliant focus and fulfillment in the Gospels' record of Jesus. Even as Jesus revealed the Father more fully than any prophet, priest, or king had done, so Jesus revealed the Holy Spirit more completely than He had ever been made known before. We should bring together the main truths Jesus taught us about the Spirit because everything else in the Bible must be understood in the light of these truths:

Jesus was begotten by the Holy Spirit in the womb of the virgin Mary.

The Holy Spirit inspired Elizabeth to pronounce a blessing upon the virgin Mary and upon the holy Child she was to bear.

The Holy Spirit prepared Simeon to recognize and proclaim the Christ Child when He was born; the Spirit led Simeon up to the Temple at exactly the right moment to see the Baby and inspired him to pronounce a marvelous blessing upon the Child.

John the Baptist was filled with the Spirit "even from his mother's womb" and was enabled to recognize Jesus as the Messiah by seeing the Spirit "descend as a dove from heaven" and remain upon Jesus. Even Zechariah, the father of John, was empowered by the Spirit to prophesy God's visitation and redemption of His people.

The Spirit came upon Jesus at His baptism to anoint Him with power for His messianic mission. The Spirit drove Jesus into the wilderness to face the tempter.

Jesus promised that the Holy Spirit would give the disciples the words to say when they were dragged before rulers and authorities.

Jesus cast out demons by the Spirit of God and warned the Pharisees that they would never be forgiven if they blasphemed the Spirit by attributing His power to Beelzebul, the prince of demons.

Jesus taught His disciples to pray for the gift of the Holy Spirit.

The resurrected Lord breathed the Holy Spirit into His disciples in order to send them forth on mission as the Father had sent Jesus into the world on mission.

Jesus declared that no one could enter the kingdom of God until that one was born again, or born from above, by the power of the Spirit.

Notes

1. For the Epistle of Gregory Nazianzus, insisting on the phrase "mother of God," see Henry Bettenson, ed., *Documents of the Christian Church* (New York and London: Oxford University Press, 1947), p. 64.

2. See ibid., for the creedal development of the doctrine of the holy Trinity, pp. 34-37.

3. Adoptionism is one of the most persistent heresies concerning the person of Christ throughout the history of Christianity. The dangers and roots of adoptionism are thoroughly discussed in G. C. Berkouwer, *The Person of Christ* (Grand Rapids: William B. Eerdmans, 1954), pp. 311-324.

4. This class of conditional sentence, assumed to be true or fulfilled, is thoroughly discussed in A. T. Robertson, *A Grammar of the Greek New Testament in the Light of Historical Research* (Nashville: Broadman Press, 1934), pp. 1007-1011.

5. See the very fine treatment of this passage in William E. Hull, "John," *The Broadman Bible Commentary* (Nashville: Broadman Press, 1970) 9:285 *ff.*

6. For a creative interpretation of this controversial passage see F. F. Bruce, *The Gospel of John* (Grand Rapids, Michigan: William B. Eerdmans, 1983), pp. 83-85.

5

Jesus and the Paraclete

The clearest teaching in all the Bible about the relationship of Jesus to the Father and the Holy Spirit is found in the Paraclete sayings in the Gospel of John. There are five of them in John 14—16, and they have a beautiful literary form which suggests to many Bible scholars that they may actually be hymns which were sung by the early church. They use the word *paraklētos* (one called alongside) for the Holy Spirit. Because they were all given by Jesus in the upper room, at the time of the Last Supper, early Christians may have sung them in connection with the observance of the Lord's Supper.

The most surprising thing about these Paraclete sayings is that they seem to take the place of the bread and the cup in John's account of the Last Supper. John described everything else about that last evening with Jesus and the disciples, the night before the cross. He mentioned the supper, the washing of the disciples' feet, and the warning about the betrayer. John recalled the departure of Judas and made the suggestive comment that when the betrayer went out of the upper room, "it was night" (John 13:30). Not only was it pitch dark in the streets of Jerusalem; it was darkest "night" in the soul of Judas!

Although John had many words that echo the Lord's Supper in his beautiful account of the feeding of the five thousand in Galilee (John 6), he had no sayings about the bread and cup at the Last Supper. He certainly implied that Jesus gave them the bread and the cup, just as the other evangelists said in their accounts; but John emphasized the presence of the Paraclete, first as Jesus, and then as indwelling Spirit. Interestingly, this is exactly what the bread and the cup meant: the signs of the powerful presence of the Lord with whom they were communing in the Lord's Supper.

The Meaning of *Paraklētos*

Bible translators go in all directions when they come to the word *paraklētos*. It probably would have been better if they had simply transliterated the Greek word straight into its English equivalent, *Paraclete*. Then the reader could, at least, have been able to discover the meaning by seeing how the word is used in the biblical context. But the King James translators chose the word *Comforter*. The Revised Standard translators chose *Counselor; The Good News Bible* translators used *Helper*. There are more than a dozen English translations, including *Teacher, Guide, Companion, Advocate,* and other synonyms. Surely the reader who is not familiar with Greek must wonder why these learned scholars do not agree!

In fact, these are all paraphrases: that is, words that illustrate possible meanings but do not translate *paraklētos* literally. It is easy to break the word down into its literal root meaning and then to examine how it is used in order to understand its meaning for us today.

The preposition *para* is well-known in English: *para*llel, *para*digm. It means "side by side," "alongside." *Klētos* is a noun which comes from the verb *kaleo,* "to call." It means, "One who is called." Put them together and you have the beautifully simple meaning "One called alongside." When Jesus promised that the Paraclete will come "alongside" us, He meant that this One called alongside us will be available to help us with our deepest need. If we are grieving, He will be our Comforter. Any Christian who has ever turned in simple faith to the Lord in the hour of grief knows the presence of the Blessed Comforter. If we are stumbling and trying to find our way, the Paraclete will be our Guide. When we are trying to understand a passage of Scripture, the same Holy Spirit who inspired it will come to be our Teacher and unfold its meaning for us. This is the glory of the wonderful Paraclete: He will come alongside us to help us in the way we need Him most.[1]

First Paraclete Saying

The first of these Paraclete Sayings is found in John 14:16-17; Jesus said,

> I will pray the Father and he will give you another Counselor, to be with you for ever, even the Spirit of truth, whom the world cannot receive, because it neither sees him nor knows him, you know him, for he dwells with you, and will be in you.

Surely, no more beautiful words were ever written! In simple and powerful language, Jesus told His disciples that the One who had been dwelling *with* them for about three years, the "Spirit of truth" or Paraclete, would come to dwell *in* them. The coming One was, in some way, identical with Jesus; He was also, in some way, different from Jesus.

Jesus Asked for the Spirit

Jesus said, "I will *pray* the Father." *Pray* is simply the little word *ask*. It is the basic word for *prayer* in every language. The Holy Spirit could not come in the way God wanted Him to come until Jesus asked for Him! Jesus had to prepare the way, call disciples to be the "temples" of the Spirit, and then ask the Father to send Him. There were no shortcuts; Jesus had to come into human history, reveal the love of the Father, call disciples to respond to that love, offer His own life for them, and then call upon the Father to send the Paraclete before He could actually come into their lives.

People cannot "get" the Spirit, manipulate the Spirit, or "work up" the Spirit. He is pure gift. He comes only by the gracious love of the Father in answer to the prayer of the obedient Son; He comes only upon the basis of the redemptive ministry of Jesus. The Father will *give* the Spirit. He cannot be deserved, bought, earned, or merited by all the good work in the history of the world. He cannot be invoked or bestowed by any religious huckster. He comes only by the sovereign grace of a loving Father in response to the prayer of Jesus.

Another Who Is Somehow the Same

The next words in this first Paraclete Saying are supremely important: Jesus said, "The Father will give you *another* Paraclete." This tells us that the disciples already had one Paraclete, namely Jesus, who was living alongside them, to help them with their deepest needs. But the word for *another* tells us something very important about the other Paraclete who would be with them when Jesus went away.

There are two words in Greek for "another": *heteron,* which means "another of a different kind." We have it in words like "heterodox," which means "another kind of thinking" or a "different kind of thinking." But Greek also has the word *allon,* which means "another of the same kind."[2] *Allon* is the word used here. The Paraclete who is coming is of the same kind of being as Jesus: that is, Divine Being! But He is also different in some way. Jesus explained how the coming Paraclete would be different from Him: "to be with you for ever." Jesus could not remain with them, in the flesh, much longer. He was about to complete His earthly mission with His death and resurrection and return to the Father. He could not abide with them "for ever." But the coming Paraclete, the Spirit of truth, could abide with them permanently.

In the Bible, as in modern physics, time and space are often correlates of each other. The Holy Spirit who is not limited by time is also not limited by space. He can be with persons anywhere, in Judea, Galilee, or the ends of the earth; and He can be with believers as long as time shall last. What a glorious promise!

The Spirit of Truth

For the first time, Jesus spelled out the name of the coming Paraclete as *Spirit:* The same Spirit who hovered over the great deep in creation, who brought the Word of God to the prophets, who begot Jesus in the virgin's womb, anointed Jesus at His baptism, and by whom He cast out demons, is the Paraclete who was coming to be with the disciples in answer to the prayer of Jesus. But this time Jesus called Him the Spirit of *truth, alētheia* in the Greek. This word for "truth" can mean what is true, rather than false, or right, rather than wrong. But its characteristic use in John's Gospel is to designate what is "real," "enduring," or "genuine," as contrasted with something which is transient or artificial.[3] The Spirit of truth, the Paraclete, will never fail; when all else passes away, He will endure forever and forever. Only those lives that are in touch with the Spirit of truth are in touch with the God who will never fade away.

Whom the World Cannot Receive

The word for "receive" in this verse is the little Greek word *labein,* which literally means to take, grasp, or seize. Metaphorically, it can mean to grasp with the mind or understand. It could have a very literal meaning here, because, in a few hours men were going to seize and bind Jesus; but they could never capture and bind the Holy Spirit. It also means that "the world," those outside the circle of believers, cannot "see" or "know" the Spirit. Nonbelievers had no personal relationship to the Spirit as the disciples did in their relationship to Jesus.

He Will Be in You

These final words of the first Paraclete Saying are so holy and so deeply moving that we feel as if we should take off our shoes and fall on our faces. This is holy ground! "You know him," Jesus said. I can almost hear Thomas mumbling under his breath, "How can we know Him? Jesus said he was going to pray to the Father and ask for the Paraclete to come. How can we know Him if he hasn't come yet?" Jesus answered the question before it was even asked: "How do you know Him? He has been dwelling with you for three years; He is dwelling with you right now!" Jesus was the Paraclete who had been alongside them throughout their years together. The One who walked around Galilee touched the blinded eyes to make them see; the One who stood before an open tomb in Bethany and said, "Lazarus, come forth!" This same Paraclete who had been "dwelling with them" all this time was coming as the Paraclete to dwell *in* them. It is overwhelming. It is abounding grace. It is beyond our minds to grasp. The Creator Word who called the worlds into being poured out His life on Calvary for us. The living Lord who broke the bars of death and came forth from the grave alive forevermore wants to live in our mortal bodies, to think through our minds, to speak through our lips, to bind up the wounded with our hands, to walk on our feet in the tragic byways of this suffering world. How could anyone carelessly defile this body, this temple of the Holy Spirit? It is the supreme miracle. The Paraclete lives in us!

Second Paraclete Saying

There is a kind of "bridge" at the end of the first Paraclete Saying. Most scholars do not include it in the Saying because it does not fit the same literary form. But it does lead into the rest of the chapter and into the second Saying: Jesus said, "I will not leave you desolate; I will come to you" (John 14:18). The word "desolate" is *orphanous,* orphans! Jesus would not leave them like little children bereft of their parents. Also, He explicitly identified Himself with the coming Paraclete. Jesus would go away, but the Spirit would come to them. Jesus would go away in His physical body, but He would come as Spirit-Paraclete to be even closer. He would *indwell* them. Then Jesus gave the second Paraclete Saying:

> These things I have spoken to you, while I am still with you.
> But the [Paraclete], the Holy Spirit, whom the Father will
> send in my name, he will teach you all things, and bring to
> your remembrance all I have said to you (John 14:15-16).

Another great truth jumps right off the page and into our hearts. The incarnation of the Son of God as the man Jesus revealed the nature of God as He had never been revealed before. But, at the same time, this embodiment of the Divine Being in the life of Jesus was subject to some severe limitations. Jesus was limited by history. He could not explain some things to the disciples because they would not understand them until after His death and resurrection. Some things could not happen until Jesus was "taken up" and the Spirit came to live in the disciples. Shocking as it may have seemed, the "going away" of Jesus would open up truth and understanding which had never been possible before because the Paraclete could teach them what the earthly Jesus was not able to teach them yet. Jesus could not unfold the fullest meaning of the cross, resurrection, ascension, and Pentecostal outpouring of the Spirit until after they had happened! The Paraclete who was coming would be able to teach them the meaning of these things, which were yet to come.

In My Name

A marvelous progression of spiritual truth takes place in the sequence of these Paraclete Sayings. In the first Jesus said that He would ask the Father and the *Father* would *give* them another Paraclete. Next, in an important theological progression, Jesus said, "Whom the Father will send *in my name.*" For understanding the doctrine of the Holy Spirit, this is profoundly important. The Holy Spirit could come only as the Father wanted Him to come, through the life and ministry of Jesus.

The Bible has no word for our word *person.* Our word comes from the Latin *persona* and did not come into theological use until well after the time of Christ. But the important concept of "personality" is carried in the Bible by the Hebrew word *Shem,* "name," and by its Greek equivalent, *onoma.* When God gave His name to Moses at the burning bush (Ex. 3), He was giving Himself in personal relationship to Moses. When David sang, "He leadeth me in the paths of righteousness for his name's sake" (Ps. 23:3), he was telling about a very personal relationship with the heavenly Shepherd. When we are baptized "into the name" of Jesus (the literal rendering of the oft-repeated New Testament phrase), we are declaring publicly a very intimate and personal relationship by which we have come into Christ and He has come into us.

Thus, the Father will send the Paraclete, the Holy Spirit, through the very person and life of Jesus. There is no other way to receive the Spirit. There is no such thing as having Jesus Christ and not having the Holy Spirit. To separate them would be to split God apart! Even as Jesus and the

Father are one, so Jesus and the Spirit are one. When the Father sends the Holy Spirit in Jesus' name, the Spirit comes through the very personality of Jesus!

He Will Bring to Your Remembrance

This Saying closes with the most powerful promise we have about the historicity and reliability of the words of Jesus, recorded in the Gospels. Jesus said, "The [Paraclete] . . . will . . . bring to your remembrance all that I have said to you." When scholars argue about whether we can trust the evangelists', Matthew's, Mark's, Luke's, and John's, written accounts of the words and deeds of Jesus, they sometimes talk as if God had gone off somewhere and disappeared from the earthly scene. We have the promise of Jesus that the same Holy Spirit who empowered His words and deeds would bring back to their memory "all that he said to them." Could there be any greater assurance? Could faith ask for anything more: that the same Holy Spirit who indwelt Jesus would indwell His followers and make His words come alive again in them? Yes, faith can have one more great assurance. That same Holy Spirit can indwell us today to bring the words of Jesus across the centuries into vibrant power in our lives.

Third Paraclete Saying

At the end of John 15, while Jesus and the eleven disciples were still at the table (Judas had gone out into the night), we hear the encouraging words of the third Paraclete Saying:

> But when the Counselor comes, whom I shall send to you from the Father, even the Spirit of truth, who proceeds from the Father, he will bear witness to me; and you also are witnesses, because you have been with me from the beginning (John 15:26-27).

Whom I Shall Send

Now the procession of the Spirit is complete. In the first Saying Jesus said: "I will ask the Father and *He will give you* another Paraclete." In the second Saying, we learned that the Father would send the Spirit *in Jesus' name.* In the third Saying, Jesus completed the cycle with these words: "Whom *I shall send to you* from the Father." Then Jesus added: "Who proceeds from the Father." Now we can understand that Jesus had to return to the presence of the Father, after the cross and resurrection, before he could "send the Spirit of truth" upon the disciples.

Emil Brunner, the Swiss theologian, used to hold up three fingers before his theology students and say something like this: "When you hold up three fingers, side by side, and let them stand for Father, Son and Holy Spirit, you are in danger of visualizing three separate gods. Turn them so your fingers are in line. Then you can visualize One God, even though you remember there are three persons."[4] And I would take this simple visual image one step further. The finger that is closest to us represents the Holy Spirit; this is the point where the being of God touches us. But it is only through the Spirit that we can come to the middle one, Jesus. We cannot see Jesus in the days of His flesh. We are brought to Jesus by the Spirit. When we are brought to Jesus by the Spirit, we then have access through Jesus to the Father. There is no other way. The "sin against the Holy Spirit" is unforgivable because when we blaspheme and drive away the Holy Spirit we have destroyed the only "point of contact" we have with God. If we reverse our look at the direction of the Spirit's procession, we see that the Father sent the Son. Then, in response to the prayer and ministry of Jesus, the Father sent the Spirit through the Son to dwell in the lives of the believers. The fullness of the Godhead confronts us in the

Father, as well as in the Son, and in the Spirit as well. You cannot have One without the Other!

The acceptance of this clear teaching of Jesus would save us from some of the terrible distortions of the doctrine of the Spirit. We would know, then, that we cannot have Jesus without having the Spirit. Only the Spirit can bring us to Jesus or to the Father. There is no such thing as a "born-again believer" in Christ who does not have the Spirit. One can be born again only by the regenerating activity of the Holy Spirit; one can be in Christ only by the Holy Spirit who brought one to Christ. Also, God is not a vindictive diety who peevishly decides that there is one sin—the sin of blasphemy against the Holy Spirit—which He will not forgive. Rather, if we decide to blaspheme and drive away the wooing Holy Spirit of God, we have destroyed the only point of contact we have with the holy God. We are doomed by our own vindictiveness, not God's!

Bearing Witness to Jesus

One of the unfortunate implications of the contemporary "rediscovery" of the Holy Spirit in many Christian congregations is that people become so obsessed with the Spirit that Jesus fades into the background. Jesus said very plainly in this third Saying, "The Spirit will bear witness to me." Any spirit which does not magnify Jesus is not the Spirit of God. John warned in his First Epistle not to believe every spirit, "But test the spirits to see whether they are of God" (1 John 4:1). John gave a simple test to determine if a spirit is the Spirit of God: "Every spirit which confesses that Jesus Christ has come in the flesh is of God" (v. 2). The Holy Spirit will *con*fess Jesus, *magnify* Jesus, *bear witness* to Jesus. A lot of spirits abroad today fail this test. John said they must be rejected as "the spirit of antichrist" (v. 3). Only the Spirit which exalts Jesus, which draws us to Jesus, is the Spirit of God!

You Also Are Witnesses

Many biblical scholars terminate the third Paraclete Saying at this point because of the literary form. But verse 27 certainly makes an application of the message of this Saying: *witnessing to Jesus.* Like the Spirit, the disciples were also to be witnesses to Jesus. The reason the Holy Spirit can bear witness to the Son, and the Son can bear witness to the Father is that they have been One with the Father from before all time. Using this relationship as an anology, Jesus reminded His disciples that they could bear witness to Him because they had been with Him from the beginning of His ministry. They could bear their witness only upon the basis of their relationship to Jesus. The reason so many church members find it difficult to bear witness to Jesus today is because they have no relationship out of which to bear this witness. We cannot share what we do not have! Witnessing is the outward expression of a very intimate and meaningful relationship.

Fourth Paraclete Saying

The fourth and fifth Paraclete Sayings in John's Gospel come right together in 16:7-11 and 16:13-14. There is only a short, one-verse "bridge" between them, verse 12. Saying four is the longest of the Paraclete Sayings, but it has a single dominant theme:

> Nevertheless I tell you the truth: it is to your advantage that I go away, for if I do not go away the Counselor will not come to you; but if I go, I will send him to you. And when he comes, he will convince the world concerning sin and righteousness and judgment: concerning sin, because they do not

believe in me; concerning righteousness, because I go to the
Father, and you will see me no more; concerning judgment,
because the ruler of this world is judged (John 16:7-11).

To a bewildered and frightened band of disciples, Jesus gave
this surprising word: "It is better for you that I go away"
(GNB). Unbelievable! How could this be? They were deva-
stated by the heavy dread that had been hanging over them
for days. Something was about to happen to Jesus. The religious leaders had been plotting His death for some time; now
they may have suspected Judas plotting with them. How
could it be *better* for Jesus to be taken away?

Better for Them

Jesus began this Saying with a very direct introductory
line: "Nevertheless I tell you the *truth*" Remembering that
"truth" in John's Gospel usually means "eternal reality," we
can understand that Jesus was putting them in touch with
the reality that cannot be shaken, no matter what happens.
At that very moment they needed the reality that would not
fail them.

Then Jesus gave them two decisive reasons it was better
for them that He was going away:

First, the Paraclete could not come until Jesus went away.
This is what we called earlier the "mutually exclusive" ministry of Jesus and the Spirit. During the days of the ministry
of Jesus, the redemptive ministry of the Holy Spirit was
concentrated in Jesus. The limitations upon the human Jesus
were obvious: He could not be with his followers in Galilee
and in Judea at the same time. Jesus had to walk nearly one
hundred rocky miles, as the road went. The Spirit would be
free to work with those crushing burdens of our human
existence without the limitation of time and space. He could
be anywhere, anytime believers gathered in Jesus' name.

Second, Jesus had to "go away," that is, back to the Father, back to the glory which He had with the Father "before the foundation of the world" (John 17:24), before He could "send the Paraclete" to them. Jesus had to complete His mission and return to the Father before the Holy Spirit could come to empower the disciples to continue the mission of Jesus in the world. They were not able to understand this then. But every true disciple of Jesus knows that this powerful activity of the Holy Spirit is the only way that the redemptive purpose of God can be carried out in this world. It is not by our power, or might, but by God's Spirit that the broken, sinful, and dying people of this world can be made whole.

Convincing the World

The other part of this Saying is directed toward assuring the disciples that when the Paraclete came, He could do something that could never be done without Him and had never been done before.

The Paraclete would convince, or convict, the world (all those outside the circle of believers) of three things:

First, He would convict the world of *sin.* Nearly always, when the word *sin* is in the singular in John it means the sin of unbelief, which is the root of all sin. The root of all our spiritual problems is the unwillingness to believe and trust utterly in the Lord! Only the Holy Spirit can convict people of this sin of not believing in Jesus. And only this sin of persistent unbelief is the absolutely fatal and irreversible pathway to eternal ruin. This is why Jesus said that the Paraclete had to come: He is the only One who can convict people and draw them to the Savior.

Second, He would convict the world of *righteousness,* Jesus said, "Because I go to the Father, and you will see me no more." As long as Jesus was with them, in the flesh, the disciples and the world could look to Jesus as their "standard of righteousness." He was the model and example for their lives. But when Jesus went away to the Father, they would have to depend upon the Spirit to bring to their remembrance what Jesus did and said. They would have to depend upon the "witness to Jesus" by the Holy Spirit to guide them in right living, in the way of righteousness.

Finally, the Paraclete would convict the world of *judgment* "because the ruler of this world is judged." By the convicting power of the Spirit, the world can see that reality is not found where most people think it is: in power, or wealth, or pleasure, or sensual gratification. All these things have been judged and found wanting in the cross of Christ. Satan has lost the decisive battle, and the outcome of the war is certain. Sacrificial love, "the Lamb that was slain," will ultimately rule the universe. Most people still believe that the ruler of this world, the one who depends upon lies, deception, greed, lust, death, and destruction, is the real power to be reckoned with. Only by the convicting work of the Holy Spirit can people see that, in fact, that evil one has already been judged and condemned. His doom is sure. To Christ belongs the ultimate victory!

Fifth Paraclete Saying

After the "bridge" of John 16:12, we come to the last Paraclete Saying. In a tender and touching word, Jesus assured His disciples that He had "many things to say"; but He knew that they could not "bear them now." Jesus had already told them that the coming Paraclete would lead them into truth that they could not possibly understand now. His compassionate concern for them knew their limits and felt their weakness. But Jesus did have a final word to lift their flagging spirits:

> When the Spirit of truth comes, he will guide you into all the truth; for he will not speak on his own authority, but whatever he hears he will speak, and he will declare to you the things that are to come. He will glorify me, for he will take what is mine and declare it to you. All that the Father has is mine; therefore I said that he will take what is mine and declare it to you (John 16:13-15).

Jesus did not have to say it all then. He could depend upon the Spirit to guide them later at the rate they were able to walk and at the depth they were able to understand. Jesus knew what many of his followers have never learned: All spiritual truth cannot be crammed into one person or into a group of believers at one time. Believers have to learn it, one step at a time. The urgency we sometimes feel to drag people all the way through in one big swoop is usually wrong. We should be much more concerned about which way they are moving than how far they have come along. The straight and narrow way *leads* to life; we do not make the journey in one great leap!

When the Spirit of Truth Comes

For the last time, Jesus used His favorite descriptive title for the Paraclete: "the Spirit of truth." It shows that Jesus wanted His disciples both then and now to think of the Spirit as the most powerful reality in their lives. The Spirit would be the truth to guide them, the power to sustain them, and the reality which would undergird their lives in this world and for all eternity. Instead of grieving over the departure of Jesus, the disciples were to be thinking about the time when the Spirit of truth would come. Even greater things could happen in their lives when He came!

He Will Guide You

Again Jesus acknowledged that the Spirit of truth would be able to do something when He came that even Jesus could not do while He was with them in the flesh. The Spirit could guide them into *all the truth*. This did not mean that Jesus was in any way inadequate as guide or teacher. It simply meant that Jesus could not be there, in the flesh, to guide them "into all the truth" after His resurrection and return to the right hand of the Father. On the basis of the ministry of Jesus, His death and resurrection, the Spirit would be able to guide them into truth and reality that had never been available to them before.

The Authority of Truth

All through the ministry of Jesus, religious hecklers demanded that He answer "by what authority" He dared to teach as He taught and worked the miracles He did. Here we have the answer. A certificate or degree from the "Seminary of the Sanhedrin" did not validate the ministry of Jesus. The power of God Himself authenticated Jesus' words and deeds.

So it is with the Spirit. He does not speak on His own authority, as if He were another god, or another spiritual power. That kind of polytheism dominates the religions of the world and has even affected some forms of Christianity. Rather it is because the Spirit participates in the very being of God that "whatever he hears he will speak." The Spirit has been One with the Father and the Son from before all time, through all eternity, forever and forever. His authority is not the authority of an independent spirit, commissioned by God to carry out a ministry; His authority is the authority of God Himself.

The Things That Are to Come

The future was very much on the mind of Jesus on the last evening before the cross. It had to be. His earthly ministry was just about to be completed, and the Paraclete would be taking up where the earthly ministry of Jesus left off. Jesus had declared many things to His disciples, things that had turned their lives around and set them on a new course. But their journey was just beginning. All along that "pilgrim journey," the Spirit would be declaring to them what they would need to know about the things they were going to face.

He Will Glorify Me

Once more Jesus emphasized the real ministry of the Spirit of truth: He would glorify Jesus, making known the innermost being of Jesus, by taking what truly belonged to Jesus and declaring it to the disciples. Only the Spirit could "declare" Jesus' death, resurrection, and ascension to the disciples and to us. Everything about Jesus is brought to us by the Spirit: Jesus' power, His love, His saving grace, His great salvation, transforming and life-giving.

All the Father Has Is Mine

These last words of the last Paraclete Saying tie together everything Jesus had been saying about the unity and interrelatedness of Father, Son, and Spirit. Everything the Father has belongs to Jesus. That is why the Spirit can take what belongs to Jesus, which is everything that belongs to the Father, and make it known to the disciples. The really shocking thing in these last words is not that everything in the being of God is shared fully by Father, Son, and Spirit. The almost unbelievable truth is that, through the Spirit of truth, this divine reality can be shared with us!

Conclusion

The five Paraclete Sayings in John's Gospel open up ave-
nues of understanding about the Spirit-Paraclete that cannot
be found anywhere else in the Bible. Without them we could
not have a full doctrine of the Holy Spirit. With their light
we can understand more clearly all the rest of the scriptural
teaching about the Spirit. Because of them, a floodlight of
spiritual truth is thrown on our own experience of the Holy
Spirit. Let us follow this "Guide . . . into all the truth" as
we study the remaining Scriptures about the Spirit and as we
try to formulate our own understanding of the Holy Spirit
in our lives.

Notes

1. For one of the best treatments of the unusual word *parakletos,*
see Johannes Behm, "*parakletos,*" *Theological Dictionary of the
New Testament,* Gerhard Kittel and Gerhard Friedrich, eds.
(Grand Rapids: William B. Eerdmans, 1967) 5: 800-814.

2. This important distinction of *allon* is fully explained by a
study of usage in Walter Bauer, *A Greek-English Lexicon of the
New Testament and Other Early Christian Literature,* W. F. Arndt
and F. W. Gingrich, trans. and ed. (Chicago: The University of
Chicago Press, 1957, 1969), p. 39.

3. Ibid. The crucial meaning of *aletheia* as *reality* in John's
Gospel, and elsewhere, is traced and illustrated on pp. 35-36.

4. Emil Brunner used this visual symbolism while discussing the
Trinity with my theology students at the Baptist Seminary in Rüs-
chlikon, Switzerland, in 1961.

6

The Spirit and the Church

In Luke's Gospel, he "dealt with all that Jesus began to do and teach" (Acts 1:1). In the sequel to his Gospel, Luke continued the story of the ministry of Jesus in the church. The same Holy Spirit who indwelt Jesus was indwelling the church and continuing the ministry of the Lord. For this reason, the Book of Acts is sometimes called the "Gospel of the Holy Spirit." It is the record of the acts of the Holy Spirit in the church.

Baptized with the Holy Spirit

John the Baptist had promised that the One coming after him would "baptize with the Holy Spirit." Jesus expressly fulfilled that promise when He said, "For John baptized with water, but before many days you shall be baptized with the Holy Spirit" (Acts 1:5). Thus Jesus identified the outpouring of the Holy Spirit upon the disciples on the Day of Pentecost as the "baptism of the Spirit" that John had promised. Peter recalled these words of Jesus as he recounted the experience of the falling of the Holy Spirit upon the believers at Caesarea:

> As I began to speak, the Holy Spirit fell on them just as on us at the beginning. And I remembered the word of the Lord, how he said, "John baptized with water, but you shall be

91

baptized with the Holy Spirit." If then God gave the same gift to them as he gave to us when we believed in the Lord Jesus Christ, who was I that I could withstand God? (Acts 11:15-17).

For the original disciples and for the believers at Caesarea, the gift of the Spirit came when they "believed in the Lord Jesus Christ." Jesus had already promised that the Holy Spirit would come upon them and that they would be His witnesses in Judea (fulfilled at Pentecost, Acts 2), in Samaria (fulfilled at Caesarea, Acts 10), and the uttermost parts of the earth (fulfilled at Ephesus, Acts 19). Each of these baptisms of the Spirit was an expansion of the mission of the church from Jewish believers in Judea, to proselyte or God-fearing Gentiles in Caesarea, to full Gentiles in Ephesus. The "baptism of the Spirit" was once for all, never repeated in the experience of these early believers. Fillings with the Spirit could later be repeated, but the baptism was always connected with their believing in the Lord Jesus Christ and their empowering for witness to Him in the world.[1]

In each of the passages about the baptism of the Spirit in the Book of Acts, several other expressions are used for the same event: "the Holy Spirit fell" on them or on all who heard (Acts 10:44; 11:15); "the gift of the Holy Spirit" (10: 45; cf. 11:17), where "gift" is always singular and means the Holy Spirit Himself, unlike Paul's later teaching about the multiple gifts of the Spirit. This baptism is also called "receiv[ing] the Holy Spirit" (10:47) and even receiving the gift of the Holy Spirit (2:38) and is always connected with believing in Jesus. The followers of John the Baptist whom Paul discovered at Ephesus had never believed on Jesus. When Paul preached Jesus to them and they were baptized in the name of the Lord Jesus, Paul laid his hands on them and the Holy Spirit came on them (19:5-6). This passage is consistent with all the other examples in Acts and throughout the New Testament.[2] Baptism of the Holy Spirit occurred when people believed on Jesus, and this baptism empowered them to be His witnesses to all the world.

Filled with the Spirit

Unlike the once-for-all baptism of the Holy Spirit, the phrase "full of the Spirit" or "filled with the Spirit" can be used to describe repeated experiences in the Christian life. It is first used in connection with the coming of the Holy Spirit at Pentecost: "They were all filled with the Holy Spirit and began to speak in other tongues" (Acts 2:4). After the initial coming of the Spirit, the word "filled" is never used again for the beginning of the Christian life but rather describes spiritual experiences along the way. Peter was "filled with the Holy Spirit" as he spoke to the rulers about the healing of the crippled man (4:8). After prayer, the meeting place of the early church was shaken, and "they were all filled with the Holy Spirit and spoke the word of God with boldness" (Acts 4:31). The seven who were chosen to serve tables were "full of the Spirit and of wisdom" (6:3), and Stephen was "full of faith and of the Holy Spirit" (v. 5). As Stephen faced the stones of the angry mob, he was "full of the Holy Spirit" (7:55).

Continuing this "Gospel of the Spirit," Luke used the phrase to carry the theme of his book: Ananias laid his hands on Saul that he might regain his sight and "be filled with the Holy Spirit" (Acts 9:17).[3] Barnabas was a "good man, full of the Holy Spirit and of faith" when he was sent to Antioch (11:24). Paul was "filled with the Holy Spirit" when the confronted Elymas (13:9).

These fillings of the Holy Spirit were related to two aspects of the Christian life: They marked the special character of certain Christians who were chosen to be leaders in the early church; they empowered Christians to witness and perform deeds that they could never have done in their own strength.

Directed by the Spirit

In the most natural way, Luke referred to the directions of the Holy Spirit in the life of the early church; but he never explained exactly how the Holy Spirit told them what to do. While the church at Antioch was worshiping the Lord and fasting, the Holy Spirit said, "Set apart for me Barnabas and Saul for the work to which I have called them" (Acts 13:2). Luke gave no explanation of how the Spirit spoke to them, but they received the message and the first missionary journey was begun. Most of us have had the opportunity to hear the gospel and believe on Jesus because the Christians at Antioch heard the Spirit and carried the gospel message to our forebears.

The brethren at the Jerusalem Council wrote a letter to the brethren of Antioch, Syria, and Cilicia, relieving them of the onerous requirements of circumcision and the law of Moses by saying, "For it has seemed good to the Holy Spirit and to us . . ." (Acts 15:28), acknowledging the presence and agreement of the Spirit as naturally as if He were one of the brethren present for the meeting.

The Spirit even directed Paul and Silas on their journey: "They went through the region of Phrygia and Galatia, having been forbidden by the Holy Spirit to speak the word in Asia" (Acts 16:6). Luke gave no details on how the Spirit communicated with them, but they had no doubt about His instructions.

The phrase Luke used at the beginning of the first missionary journey characterizes the whole mission of the church in the world both then and now: "So, being sent out by the Holy Spirit . . ." (Acts 13:4). The church is sent out on mission by the Holy Spirit.

Within the internal life of the church, the Spirit also directed activities. In his moving address to the elders of Ephesus, who came to meet Paul at Miletus, he said: "Take heed to yourselves and to all the flock, in which the Holy Spirit has made you overseers" (Acts 20:28). In the same address, Paul told them, "The Holy Spirit testifies to me in every city that imprisonment and afflictions await me" (v. 23). Thus the selection of church leaders, as well as the direction of their ministry, was attributed to the Holy Spirit.

The Spirit and the Scriptures

In a phrase that is characteristic of all the New Testament writers, Paul said to his hearers in Rome: "The Holy Spirit was right in saying to your fathers through Isaiah the prophet . . ." (Acts 28:25). It is hard to imagine a simpler or more profound view of the inspiration of Holy Scripture. The Holy Spirit spoke through the human writer. Every effort to adorn that with human words and explain the miracle detracts from the powerful simplicity of God's Word.

Thus, in the brief compass of the Book of Acts, Luke gave us a rich doctrine of the Holy Spirit for individual believers and for the church: Believers are baptized with the Holy Spirit when they believe on the Lord Jesus Christ; they are filled with the Spirit to accomplish the tasks given to them and to witness to Jesus; they are directed by the Spirit in every step of their Christian mission in the world; and the Spirit speaks through the writers of Holy Scripture to us today. No commentary can improve upon this simple and comprehensive doctrine of the Spirit.

Notes

1. Donald M. Joy has given us a good set of biblical definitions for "baptism of the Spirit," "infilling of the Spirit," "sanctification" and other terms in his book, *The Holy Spirit and You* (New York: Abingdon Press, 1965), pp. 113 *ff.*

2. For an excellent treatment of this difficult passage on the disciples of John the Baptist, see T. C. Smith, "Acts" *The Broadman Bible Commentary* (Nashville: Broadman Press, 1970) 10:110.

3. Some interpreters might argue that the term "filled with the Holy spirit" is here applied to Paul's conversion. But most Bible readers consider the account of Paul's experience on the Damascus road to be his conversion and the later "filling" and the recovery of his sight to be a part of his Christian experience of preparation to be a witness to the Christ he had been fighting. In any case, these two terms are used in separate and distinctive ways: "baptism of the Spirit" marks the beginning of the Christian journey; "fillings" of the Spirit mark special times of enduement with the Spirit's power for particular missions.

7

Paul's Theology of the Spirit

The writings of Paul, which fill a large part of our New Testament, have enriched our understanding of every Christian doctrine. The doctrine of the Holy Spirit is no exception. Paul referred to the person and activity of the Holy Spirit in more than a hundred passages. Because it is impossible to treat each one individually, I will set forth the major themes in Paul's doctrine of the Spirit, illustrating his teaching by examples from his many letters. In this way we can concentrate on the new ideas Paul added to the already rich and varied biblical teaching about the Holy Spirit.

One important distinction needs to be made at the very beginning of our study of Paul's treatment of the Spirit. More than any other biblical writer, Paul referred to his spirit and to the human spirit in each person. He often characterized the totality of the human being as "spirit and soul and body" (as in the benediction in 1 Thess. 5:23). This is Paul's acknowledgment of the creative activity of God's Spirit in every human being; it is the "image of God" in the human personality. But this is very clearly the human spirit and not the Holy Spirit. For this reason, we will concentrate on the divine activity of the Holy Spirit and will not develop Paul's full doctrine of human personality.

Also, Paul had a kind of chronology of the Holy Spirit in the life of the Christian. Although he did not always carry

97

the sequence through rigidly, at times certain actions of the Holy Spirit must precede others. I will call attention to those relationships where it seemed important to Paul.

Made Alive by the Spirit

In a passage that is reminiscent of the Paraclete Sayings, Paul declared that Jesus is designated the Son of God in power, by the Holy Spirit, in His resurrection from the dead (Rom. 1:4). Then he argued that "he who raised Christ Jesus from the dead will give life to your mortal bodies also through his Spirit which dwells in you" (8:11). The Spirit who raised Jesus from the dead will raise us from the dead, and the proof of that promise is that the Spirit dwells in us now. A closely related idea is found in Galatians 4:29 where, in the analogy to Isaac and Ishmael, Christians are born of the Spirit rather than of the flesh. This is obviously the same idea as "made alive in the Spirit," but it is not developed extensively as it is in John.

Baptized by One Spirit

Echoing the words of John the Baptist and Jesus, Paul asserted that "by one Spirit we were all baptized into one body—Jews or Greeks, slaves or free—and all were made to drink of one Spirit" (1 Cor. 12:13). This is equivalent to being "born of the Spirit" or "made alive by the Spirit," but Paul used it to stress the unity of all kinds of Christians because they have all been baptized by the one Spirit. In the Gospels and in Acts, baptism by the Spirit is the sign of the Messiah, the inauguration of His ministry, and the empowering of His disciples to carry on His ministry. In Paul, it is God's way of unifying the broken and fragmented humanity into one new people of God!

Walking in the Spirit

One of the most distinctive contributions of Paul to the doctrine of the Spirit is his continuing emphasis upon "walking in the Spirit." As a devout Hebrew, Paul had been brought up in the law of *Halakah,* which means "walking." It was the sacred name for the practical instructions of the law concerning the daily walk of life.[1] How natural it was for him to substitute the liberating "law of the Spirit" for the old law "of sin and death":

> For the law of the Spirit of life in Christ Jesus has set me free from the law of sin and death. For God has done what the law, weakened by the flesh, could not do: sending his own Son in the likeness of sinful flesh and for sin, he condemned sin in the flesh, in order that the just requirement of the law might be fulfilled in us, who walk not according to the flesh but according to the Spirit (Rom. 8:2-4).

Paul also issued this challenge as direct imperative of the Christian life: "But I say, walk by the Spirit, and do not gratify the desires of the flesh" (Gal. 5:16). Paul's theology was so practical that he believed the real evidence that one had been made alive by the Spirit was the way one lived in daily life: "If we live by the Spirit, let us also walk by the Spirit" (v. 25). This integrates spiritual talk with spiritual walk. It combines doctrinal theology with ethical conduct.

Witness of the Spirit

In the great eighth chapter of Romans, where Paul developed an entire doctrine of the Holy Spirit, the role of the Spirit in making us children of God in contrast to the old spirit of slavery in sin enables us to call God "Abba! Father!" (v. 15). This is the childish word for *Daddy* or *Papa* in the Hebrew home. It is the name by which Jesus addressed God the Father, and it is the name Jesus taught His disciples to use when they prayed. This childlike prayer, Paul said, "is the Spirit himself bearing witness with our spirit that we are children of God" (v. 16).

In John's Gospel Jesus stressed the witness of the Spirit to Jesus as the Son of God. Now Paul, in a parallel way, emphasized the witness of the Spirit to our own spirits, confirming that we are the children of God. The witness of the Spirit points both ways: toward Jesus and toward us.

"First Fruits" of the Spirit

Carrying forward this same theme, Paul related it to the blessed hope of the resurrection of our bodies and eternal fellowship in the family of God: "We know that the whole creation has been groaning in travail together until now; and not only the creation, but we ourselves, who have the first fruits of the Spirit, groan inwardly as we wait for adoption as sons, the redemption of our bodies" (Rom. 8:22-23). Here the "first fruits" means the presence of the Spirit in our lives as a kind of downpayment and guarantee that the full measure will come at the resurrection of the body at the end of time. A similar idea is expressed in the *arrabon* or earnest of the Spirit, a word which also referred to an amount of "earnest money" that was paid to guarantee that the full principal would be paid at the appointed time: "He has put his seal upon us and given us his Spirit in our hearts as a guarantee" (*arrabon*, 2 Cor. 1:22).[2] In other words, our Christian assurance is grounded in the presence and witness of the Holy Spirit. Paul believed that the Christian life ought to bring assurance and liberation, rather than the fear and slavery of the law. The Holy Spirit is the power that brings this confidence and liberation to the Christian.

This same idea is expressed in Ephesians 1:13-14. Paul told his readers that they "were sealed with the promised Holy Spirit, which is the guarantee [*arrabon*] of our inheritance until we acquire possession of it." In all these passages the Holy Spirit is a foretaste of the full inheritance Christians will receive when Jesus comes. The eschatological (end-time) reward is already being experienced by the presence of the Holy Spirit. This is equivalent to John's doctrine of eternal life, which we experience by believing in Jesus now. It also supports and complements Paul's other emphasis upon the witness of the Spirit.

Intercession by the Spirit

In the great chapter on the Spirit in Romans 8, Paul came to another activity of the Spirit, which no other writer emphasized in the same way: "Likewise the Spirit helps us in our weakness; for we do not know how to pray as we ought, but the Spirit himself intercedes for us with sighs too deep for words" (v. 26). The author of Hebrews reminded us that Jesus is living to make intercession for us, but Paul was affirming that the Spirit helps us when we do not know how to pray or what words to use. The Spirit's intercession goes beyond words, and Paul explained why the intercession is so effective: "And he who searches the hearts of men knows what is the mind of the Spirit, because the Spirit intercedes for the saints according to the will of God" (Rom. 8:27). Jesus had demonstrated that the deepest level of prayer was to pray that the Father's will be done, as Jesus had prayed in Gethsemane. Now the Spirit who understands the will of God perfectly can intercede for us in perfect harmony with Him who "searches the hearts of men."

The Lord Is the Spirit

Most of the passages in Paul's letters describe the activity or work of the Holy Spirit. But Paul made a few references to the person of the Holy Spirit, who the Spirit is. In 2 Corinthians 3:17, Paul directly identified the Spirit with the risen Lord: "Now the Lord is the Spirit, and where the Spirit of the Lord is, there is freedom." "Lord" was Paul's regular title for Jesus. Paul intended for us to understand that where the Spirit is present the resurrected Lord Jesus is also present.

This is one of the most important contributions to the understanding of the Holy Spirit. The Bible warns that many spirits have gone out into the world, and we need to test the spirits to be sure that they are from God. With the identification Paul made, we can know the person and character of the Spirit: He is the Spirit of Christ. The same incarnate Lord Jesus who revealed the nature of the Father also reveals the nature of the Holy Spirit. It is the best test we could have to determine if a certain spiritual activity is really the activity of the Spirit of the Lord.

In this same passage, Paul assured the Corinthians that they were being changed into the Lord's likeness "from one degree of glory to another; for this comes from the Lord who is the Spirit" (2 Cor. 3:18). The Spirit is making us more like Jesus, one step at a time, because the Lord Himself is the Spirit who is accomplishing this change in us.

In Philippians 1:19, Paul identified the Spirit with Christ in another way: "Yes, and I shall rejoice. For I know that through your prayers and the help of the Spirit of Jesus Christ this will turn out for my deliverance." Here the Spirit of the Lord, or the Holy Spirit, is simply called the "Spirit of Jesus Christ," leaving no doubt whatsoever about the identity of the Spirit. Also, Paul related prayer and the Spirit in a powerful way. Instead of the Spirit making intercession for us, Paul saw prayer as opening a channel through which the Spirit could work for Paul's deliverance from prison. Thus, prayer enables the Spirit of Christ to work and accomplish miracles which apparently could not be accomplished apart from our prayers. This is a powerful new motivation for prayer: When we fail to pray, we block the channel of the Spirit's working; when we do pray, the Spirit works through that prayer channel to accomplish God's purpose in our lives.

This may also throw light on the difficult and disputed passage in 1 Corinthians 14:14-15, where Paul contrasted "pray[ing] with the spirit" and "pray[ing with the] mind."[3] Even when we do not fully understand some human problem or need, and our minds cannot formulate exactly the right words, the Spirit may make "intercession for us with groanings which are beyond words" (Rom. 8:26, author). One thing is certain. When we are impressed to pray for someone or some need, we must not be guilty of the sin of omission by failing to pray for them. Our failure to pray may block the channel of the Spirit's working and hinder the purpose of God.

The Temple of the Spirit

Paul made his strongest plea for the purity of our bodies, keeping them free from immorality and defilement, by using the analogy of the Temple. In the Old Testament, the people believed that God's presence or *Shekinah* was dwelling in the holy of holies in the Temple. Paul took that example and reminded the Corinthians that they should not defile their bodies with sexual immorality or any other evil conduct: "Do you not know that your body is a temple of the Holy Spirit within you, which you have from God? You are not your own; you were bought with a price. So glorify God in your body" (1 Cor. 6:19-20). Paul used the term "your bodies" in this context, showing that each Christian is an individual temple in whom the Spirit dwells; but he also used *your* (plural in Greek) body to show that the church is collectively the temple of the Holy Spirit. Because of the price that

Christ paid in His atonement, the Spirit has an absolute claim upon us. We do not own ourselves; we belong to Him!

The Fruit of the Spirit

We have already seen that Paul used the "first fruits" of the Spirit to mean that the presence of the Holy Spirit is a sign and guarantee that the full measure of the promises of God will be received when Christ comes at the end of time. But when Paul used the singular "fruit" of the Spirit, he meant something entirely different. The "first fruits" always appeared long before the real harvesttime, but they were a sure sign that the full harvest would come in its proper time. But when he used the singular word "fruit," Paul was using the analogy of the growing plant in another way. The fruit is what identifies the plant and also what passes on its life into other plants. Paul named that fruit of the Spirit with one word: *agape,* the self-giving love of God. Paul surrounded the word *love* with many explanatory synonyms, but he said the *fruit* (singular) of the *Spirit* (singular) *is* (singular) *love* (singular): "But the fruit of the Spirit is love, joy, peace, patience, kindness, goodness, faithfulness, gentleness, self-control; against such there is no law" (Gal. 5:22). Love is the singular fruit of the Spirit. Every other word Paul used, *joy, peace, patience, kindness,* and all the others are words which express how love acts in our lives. They are love in action, and they are the Spirit bearing fruit in our lives.

Gifts of the Spirit

Although Paul spoke of only one *fruit* of the Spirit, he almost always spoke of a variety of *gifts* of the Spirit. Paul liked to stress the variety of gifts that came from the same Spirit. One of the great passages on the gifts of the Spirit is 1 Corinthians 12:4-6: "Now there are varieties of gifts, but the same Spirit; and there are varieties of service, but the same Lord; and there are varieties of working, but it is the same God who inspires them all in every one." Notice the Trinitarian pattern: Spirit, Lord (Paul's regular name for Jesus), God. One God is the source of the inspiration for each and every gift in every person, acting through the Lord Jesus and through the Spirit.

But gifts of the Spirit are not given for the private use and edification of the individual believers. They are given for the "common good," for the benefit of the whole church: "To each is given the manifestation of the Spirit for the common good" (1 Cor. 12:7). As we examine the list of spiritual gifts in this passage, we can see that each is designed to bring help and blessing to the church. These gifts are for ministry and service, not for private spiritual pride:

> To one is given through the Spirit the utterance of wisdom, and to another the utterance of knowledge according to the same Spirit, to another faith by the same Spirit, to another gifts of healing by the one Spirit, to another the working of miracles, to another prophecy, to another the ability to distinguish between spirits, to another various kinds of tongues, to another the interpretation of tongues. All these are inspired by one and the same Spirit, who apportions to each one individually as he wills (1 Cor. 12:8-11).

The proof that Paul saw the gifts of the Spirit as God's provision for building up the church can be found in an analysis of these gifts. Every gift contributes to the whole fellowship of the church, rather than exalting the individual who has the gift. If there were any doubt about this, Paul removed it with his direct command: "Since you are eager for manifestations of the Spirit, strive to excel in building up the church" (1 Cor. 14:12). When any effort is made to evaluate spiritual gifts, the real test is how much they build up or edify the church.

Quenching the Spirit

Just as Paul warned about the danger of undisciplined excesses in the display of spiritual gifts, he also warned about a danger in the opposite direction: "Do not quench the Spirit" (1 Thess. 5:19). The effort to restrict and control excesses could easily result in a stifling of the genuine activity of God's Spirit. Paul often tried to find a way between such extremes, as he faced theological issues in the churches. He was eminently practical and gave this good advice: "Test everything: hold fast what is good" (v. 21). There is no way to improve on that advice, as we face problems in our churches.

Sanctification by the Spirit

Paul's doctrine of salvation is often interpreted as centering in "justification by faith alone," the great theme of Martin Luther in the Reformation. That is a major theme of Paul's Roman letter, but he also emphasized that salvation is through sanctification by the Spirit: "God chose you from the beginning to be saved, through sanctification by the Spirit and belief in the truth" (2 Thess. 2:13). The word *sanctify* means "to be set apart"; the Spirit sets us apart to a different kind of life, obedient to God who chose us from the beginning to serve Him. This makes salvation, not just a transaction that is finished and left behind, but a new life that is lived in the power of the Spirit. Salvation is not a new status that is static, but a new relationship that is dynamic and growing in the Spirit.

Vindicated in the Spirit

One other facet of the activity of the Spirit is unique to the letters of Paul. In what many scholars believe to be an early Christian hymn,[4] the summary of belief in Jesus is expressed:

> He was manifested in the flesh,
> vindicated in the Spirit,
>   seen by angels,
> preached among the nations,
> believed on in the world,
>   taken up in glory (1 Tim. 3:16).

This is in line with what Paul said in the opening verses of Romans, where Jesus is declared to be the Son of God with power by the Holy Spirit in His resurrection from the dead. Here, "vindicated in the Spirit" means exactly the same thing: Although despised and crucified by men, He was vindicated by God when the Holy Spirit raised Him from the dead.

With this concept of the vindication of Jesus by the Holy Spirit in His resurrection from the dead, we have come full circle in Paul's doctrine of the Spirit. We began with the opening verses of Romans in which Paul said that Jesus was declared to be the Son of God with power when He was raised from the dead by the Holy Spirit. In this concluding doctrinal hymn in 1 Timothy, Paul declared that Jesus was vindicated by the Spirit in His resurrection, preached among the nations, believed on in the world, and taken up into glory. It gives us the opportunity for a comprehensive statement of Paul's teaching about the Spirit.

Paul's Comprehensive View of the Spirit

God is Spirit. God is Lord. God is Father. These are Paul's favorite terms for identifying the person of God. Paul often used them together when describing the various activities of the one Holy God in His work of redemption. The Spirit is the invisible but powerful presence of God, working in the creation, but especially working in the redemptive ministry of Christ. The Spirit raised Jesus from the dead, came upon the church and empowered it to proclaim salvation in Jesus' name, saved and sanctified those who believed in Jesus, enabled them to walk in the Spirit, sealed them until the day of redemption.

The Spirit continues to make intercession for us and through us, especially in our prayer life, and gives us the earnest or assurance that God will complete His purpose of redemption in our future resurrection from the dead. The Spirit pours out gifts upon us to be used in the building up of the church, in faithful ministry to the fellow church members and to the world. We should not quench the Spirit or grieve the Spirit; we should be filled with the Spirit, walk in the Spirit, and take up the "sword of the Spirit" (Eph. 6:17), which is the word of God by which we can win the victory in our battle against the powers of evil. The Spirit who vindicated Jesus will go with us all the way until we stand on that great day of redemption in the presence of the Father.

This is the most comprehensive doctrine of the Holy Spirit found in the entire Bible. It has shaped our Christian doctrine of the Spirit, through the centuries of church history, more than any other.

Notes

1. An alternative spelling of *Halakah* is *Halachah*. A fine, brief article under this heading is found in *The Interpreter's Dictionary of the Bible* (Nashville: Abingdon, 1962) 2: 512.

2. Johannes Behm, "*arrabon*," *Theological Dictionary of the New Testament*, Gerhard Kittel and Gerhard Friedrich, eds. Grand Rapids: William B. Eerdmans, 1964) 1: 475.

3. An excellent treatment of this difficult passage may be found in Raymond Bryan Brown, "1 Corinthians," *The Broadman Bible Commentary* (Nashville: Broadman Press, 1970) 10: 377.

4. Scholars such as Hans Lietzmann have defined these Christian hymns by observing their exact poetic meter, for chanting or singing, their obvious insertion into a text which is prose, and sometimes even their rhyme as in the hymns to which we are accustomed. Like a preacher who catches up the theme of his message in the familiar words of a hymn, Paul and other New Testament writers would drive home their point by appealing to the words of a beloved hymn with which their readers would be familiar.

8

The Spirit in the Other Epistles and Revelation

Only a few references to the Spirit are found in the remaining books of the New Testament. Some of these reinforce the teaching that we have already found in the Gospels, Acts, and Paul's writings. But a few of them add distinctive new insights to the unfolding doctrine of the Spirit in Holy Scripture. They are essential for a complete doctrine of the Spirit.

Hebrews

Because Hebrews interprets the redemptive ministry of Jesus against the background of the Old Testament priesthood and sacrifice, it places very limited emphasis upon the Spirit. It does have general references to "ministering spirits sent forth to serve" (1:14), but these are first angels and secondarily prophets and servants of God who go forth in the world to do His bidding.[1] However, two distinctive teachings about the Holy Spirit should not be overlooked:

Through the Eternal Spirit

After a detailed description of the animal sacrifices in the Old Testament ritual, the author of Hebrews contrasted the sacrifice of Christ:

> For if the sprinkling of defiled persons with the blood of goats
> and bulls and with the ashes of a heifer sanctifies for the

purification of the flesh, how much more shall the blood of Christ, who through the eternal Spirit offered himself without blemish to God, purify your conscience from dead works to serve the living God (9:13-14).

The contrast is striking. The Spirit empowers the offering of Christ in a way that was not possible for the animal sacrifices. Also, the "eternal Spirit" suggests that the sacrifice of Christ was permanent and final in a way that was impossible for the temporary sacrificial system. This teaching reaffirms what Paul and others had said about the work of the Holy Spirit in the redemptive ministry of Jesus.

Outraging the Spirit

Hebrews has a teaching that is remarkably close to the teaching of Jesus in the Gospels about blaspheming the Holy Spirit, or committing the unpardonable sin: "How much worse punishment do you think will be deserved by the man who has spurned the Son of God, and profaned the blood of the covenant by which he was sanctified, and outraged the Spirit of grace?" (10:29) Since Jesus offered His sacrifice in the power of the Holy Spirit and since the Spirit is the only One who can make that sacrifice effective in the life of the sanctified believer, one who has "spurned the Son of God" also outrages the Spirit of grace and destroys any possibility of salvation.[2] This outraging of the Spirit is surely equivalent to blaspheming the Spirit, and it is unpardonable because there is no other way by which we can be brought to God. The one who rejects the Spirit totally seals his or her own doom because that one has "spurned the Son of God."

First Peter

Every reference to the Holy Spirit in 1 Peter can be paralleled in Paul. There is a remarkable similarity in their teach-

ing about the Holy Spirit. In this brief epistle there are four
such references.

Sanctified by the Spirit

In a Trinitarian salutation, which would fit beautifully into
a Pauline epistle, Peter greeted the "exiles of the Dispersion"
who were "chosen and destined by God the Father and
sanctified by the Spirit for obedience to Jesus Christ and for
sprinkling with his blood" (1:1-2).

As in all the other Trinitarian salutations and benedictions
in the New Testament, the unity of the One God is assumed;
but the distinct activity of the Father, the Spirit, and Jesus
Christ in the work of redemption is distinguished very clearly. The Father chose or elected them. The Spirit sanctified
them or set them apart for their new life of obedience to
Christ whose blood "sprinkled," as in the Old Testament
ritual, was the basis of their redemption. Again, consistent
with every reference in Paul, and throughout the New Testament, the distinctive role of the Spirit is to sanctify, or set
apart, to the new life in Christ.

The Spirit of Christ

We have seen that Paul made an explicit identification of
the Holy Spirit as the Spirit of Christ. But Peter went further
by declaring that the Spirit of Christ worked in the prophets
of the Old Testament: "The prophets who prophesied of the
grace that was to be yours searched and inquired about this
salvation; they inquired what person or time was indicated
by the Spirit of Christ within them when predicting the
sufferings of Christ and the subsequent glory" (1:10-11).
Peter identified the Spirit in the Old Testament as the Spirit
of Christ because he knew that the same God who inspired
the prophets indwelt Christ in His sufferings. Paul identified
the Spirit with the risen Lord; Peter carried the identification

back to the Old Testament prophets. It is a powerful witness to the unity of the one God from the Old Covenant to the New, from the prophets to Jesus, from Paul and Peter to us.

Made Alive in the Spirit

Peter mentioned Christ's preaching to the "spirits in prison" between Good Friday and Easter morning: "For Christ also died for sins once for all, the righteous for the unrighteous, that he might bring us to God, being put to death in the flesh but made alive in the spirit; in which he went and preached to the spirits in prison" (3:18-19). Because Peter contrasted the death of Jesus in the flesh with being made alive in the spirit, he may have been simply contrasting the fleshly life of Christ before His death with His ministry in the spirit to the dead (spirits in prison) who had lived in the time of Noah. Peter identified the human spirit of Christ, in contrast to His body of flesh which remained in Joseph's tomb, as the preacher to these disobedient spirits. It was a crucial ministry of Christ to bring the Old Testament people under the one plan of redemption, whether in judgment or salvation. Peter said, "This is why the gospel was preached even to the dead, that though judged in the flesh like men, they might live in the spirit like God" (4:6). There is one way of salvation, through Jesus Christ. Those who looked forward to His coming in faith are judged on the same basis as those who lived after His coming: responding to the proclamation of the gospel of Christ who was coming, did come, and is coming again! Christ is the same, yesterday, today, and forever.

Spirit of Glory and of God

Peter encouraged Christians to face persecution courageously because they could count on the presence of the Spirit: "If you are reproached for the name of Christ, you are blessed, because the spirit of glory and of God rests upon you" (4:14). We have already seen that "glory" means the outward expression of the innermost nature of God. Christians have the opportunity to show forth the true nature of Christ as the Spirit rests upon them when they bear reproach for Christ's sake.

From the brief letter of 1 Peter, we learn that the Spirit of Christ was active in the Old Testament prophets, that Christ was "made alive" in the Spirit to proclaim the gospel even to the dead, that Christians are sanctified by the Spirit on the basis of the atoning sacrifice of Jesus, and that the Spirit of God rests upon Christians as they endure reproach for the name of Jesus. Through the one Spirit, Peter tied together the Old and New Testament, the prophets and Christ, the living and the dead, Christ and the believer, the here and the hereafter.

First John

In just three or four references, the little letter of 1 John makes an additional contribution to our understanding of the Spirit:

Known by the Spirit

One of the primary themes of 1 John is the question of knowing or recognizing whether one is really a child of God. In 1 John 3:24 John assured his readers that "by this we know that he abides in us, by the Spirit which he has given us." Christian assurance comes from the indwelling Spirit of God. But this abiding is a double abiding, we in Him and He in us: "By this we know that we abide in him and he in us, because he has given us of his own Spirit" (4:13). John anticipated the obvious question: How can one be sure that it is the Spirit of God who indwells one's life? John's answer to this question involves a testing of the spirits.

Testing the Spirits

John gave us the clearest possible way of identifying the Spirit of God:

> Beloved, do not believe every spirit, but test the spirits to see whether they are of God; for many false prophets have gone out into the world. By this you know the Spirit of God: every spirit which confesses that Jesus Christ has come in the flesh is of God, and every spirit which does not confess Jesus is not of God. This is the spirit of antichrist, of which you heard that it was coming, and now it is in the world already (1 John 4:1-3).

John had to face many people in the first century who denied that Jesus was a real flesh-and-blood man. This heretical doctrine was called Docetism, from the Greek word for "seem" or "appear." Because all flesh was evil to them, Jesus could only have appeared to be flesh.[3] John's test of the true Spirit of God was this: one must confess that Jesus, the Son of God, came in the flesh. The humanity of Jesus is just as important as the deity of Jesus. Only because He was both human and divine could He be our Savior.

The Spirit Is the Witness

Not only does the Spirit bear witness that we are children of God but he also bears witness to Christ as the Son of God: "And the Spirit is the witness, because the Spirit is the truth. There are three witnesses, the Spirit, the water, and the blood; and these three agree" (5:7-8). Most interpreters understand the water and the blood to refer to baptism and the Lord's Supper, and there is no doubt that they are signs that bear witness to Christ. But neither of them could bring conviction of the saving power of Christ without the activity of God. The Spirit works through these signs to bear witness to the Son.

Thus, for John the primary role of the Spirit was as witness. He witnesses to us that we are the children of God. He bears witness to the humanity of Christ by insisting that He came in the flesh. And He bears witness to the divine Sonship of Jesus through the signs of the water and the blood.

Revelation

The final book of the Bible has provoked debate and disagreement since it was written. It was debated for four centuries before it was finally included in the canon of Holy Scripture. The references to the Spirit in Revelation have also provoked some debate. It is important that we examine them and see what they add to our understanding of the Spirit.

The Seven Spirits Before the Throne

In the very early verses of Revelation, John addressed the seven churches of Asia: "Grace to you and peace from him who is and who was and who is to come, and from the seven spirits who are before his throne, and from Jesus Christ the faithful witness" (1:4). Interpreters go in all directions.[4] Some think the "seven spirits" are the same as the messengers or angels of the seven churches. But John carefully distinguished between angels and spirits in this book, and he would certainly not put them in between God and Jesus Christ in any case. Some have tried to bring in Iranean astrology, which counted the five planets, plus the sun and moon, as seven celestial spirits. Again, this would be a shocking and inconsistent interpolation of a foreign astrology into John's theology.

Much more likely is the view, consistent with the entire Book of Revelation, that John has used the number seven to affirm the fullness of the Spirit, the manifold activities of the One Spirit of God. It is certain from this text that God is acting through these spiritual powers. With God on the throne, the spiritual powers before the throne, and Jesus Christ the faithful witness, we have the consistent New Testament emphasis upon the Triune activity of God. From this insight we have a strong affirmation of the manifold activity of God's Spirit.

In the Spirit

Several times John used the expression "in the Spirit" (1:10; 4:2; 17:3). It means that John was caught up or empowered by the Spirit. Sometimes he was carried away in a vision by the Spirit. This is a familiar role of the Spirit, from the prophets of the Old Testament, to Jesus, Paul, and throughout the New Testament. The Spirit is the power and presence of God overwhelming and controlling the one who is caught up "in the Spirit."

Hear What the Spirit Says

Several times, especially in his letters to the churches, John interjected these words: "He who has an ear, let him hear what the Spirit says to the churches" (2:7,11,17,29; 3:6,13, 22). John plainly identified the words he wrote as "what the Spirit says." It is a powerful statement of the inspiration of the Scriptures. These words are simply what the Spirit says!

The Spirit and the Bride

The final reference to the Spirit in the Bible is the beautiful invitation of the Spirit and the Bride to the messianic banquet in heaven: "The Spirit and the Bride say, 'Come'" (22:17). The banquet is for the Son, the Anointed One or Messiah. But the Spirit anointed Him, and the same Spirit brings us to the Son in faith believing. This is why the Spirit joins in the final invitation to the heavenly banquet.

We have come full circle. The same Holy Spirit who brought the breath of life into human beings, who empowered Jesus and raised Him from the dead, and who brings faithful believers unto Him, is now ushering them into the heavenly home. The Spirit's ministry is complete!

Notes

1. For an extensive treatment of these "ministering spirits," angels, winds, and flames of fire, see Simon J. Kistemaker, *Hebrews* (Grand Rapids: Baker Book House, 1984), pp. 40 *ff.*

2. On the seriousness of this warning, see Charles A. Trentham, *"Hebrews," The Broadman Bible Commentary* (Nashville: Broadman Press, 1972) 12:76.

3. John Knox, "Docetism," *The Interpreter's Dictionary of the Bible* (Nashville: Abingdon Press, 1962), p. 860.

4. Several of these differing views are summarized by Morris Ashcraft, *"Revelation," The Broadman Bible Commentary* (Nashville: Broadman Press, 1972), 12:258.

9

A Comprehensive Doctrine of the Person and Work of the Holy Spirit

After an extensive study of the Holy Spirit in all of the biblical literature, we are now in a position to summarize a comprehensive doctrine of the person and work of the Holy Spirit and relate this statement to other Christian doctrines. Too often we begin our systematic statements of Christian doctrine by expounding the creeds of the church. But for those who accept the authority of Holy Scripture in all matters of faith and practice, the only proper way to begin is with a careful study of the biblical text. The Scripture begins with the Spirit's relation to God and then proceeds to describe the Spirit's activity; therefore, that basic principle of arrangement will be followed in summarizing the doctrine of the Spirit. As far as possible, all the categories for organizing the comprehensive statement will be drawn from the Scriptures themselves.

The Spirit of God

The very first reference to the Spirit in the Bible gives the name Spirit and the Spirit's relation to God, "of God" or "belonging to God." This is the place to begin a theological definition of the person of the Holy Spirit. The name implies person. Therefore, the Holy Spirit is the personal Spirit of God.

God, Himself, Is Spirit

God is not material, does not have a body, and is not restricted to any particular place. In this sense, everything about God is Spirit, defining the nature of God as contrasted with the physical world. But this use of the word *Spirit* to describe the nature of God does not begin to cover the personal meaning applied to the Holy Spirit in creation, in redemption, in relation to Jesus, and in relation to us as believers. For this we have to move from concepts, such as nature or character, to the concept of *person*.

The Holy Spirit Is the Power of God

As the power of God, the Spirit goes forth to create and sustain this universe, to communicate with God's creatures, to call and regenerate human beings into the spiritual family of God. We have seen that the fundamental biblical names for the threefold being of God, which later are revealed as Father, Son, and Spirit, can be found in analogy in the opening verses of the Bible: God (the Creator); Word (God spoke, "Let there be . . ."); and Spirit (hovering over the primeval creation).

The analogy to human speech is obvious. When we speak, the very breath by which we live goes forth, carrying our word, which is something of our very selves being communicated to others. God goes forth into creation and throughout the long history of His redemptive activity through His Word, borne by His Spirit. Word and Spirit take on personal characteristics, as the biblical story unfolds. Because they go forth from God, they can sometimes be distinguished from God and, at other times, identified with God. This oneness of Being and yet distinction of personalities in the Divine Mystery leads to the later doctrine of the Trinity.

It is accepted by faith even when it cannot be rationally explained.

We can now give a comprehensive definition of the person of the Holy Spirit: The Holy Spirit is the personal power and presence of God, who goes forth in conjunction with the Divine Word to create and sustain the universe, to communicate God's own Being to His creatures, and to regenerate them into a new creation. In this dynamic activity and relationship, there is personal intercommunication between the Spirit, the sending Father, and the redeeming Son.

Two Spheres of the Spirit

The moment the Bible introduces the personal Being of the Spirit and the Spirit's relation to God, it moves on to the activity of the Spirit. This is the logical sequence: first the Person and then the work, or activity. The first sphere of activity was in the creation. This creative activity of the Spirit is seen at three different levels: first, the Spirit is active in bringing creation into existence; second, the Spirit is active in sustaining the creation at every moment. If the Spirit were withdrawn, creation would collapse. Third, the biblical teaching also sets forth the magnificent vision of the Spirit's activity in bringing about a new creation, a new heaven and a new earth.

In striking parallel to this creative activity of the Spirit is the sphere of the Spirit's activity in redemption. The Spirit of God regenerates or gives new spiritual life to the one who is born into the family of God. The Spirit also sustains and empowers the newborn Christian to live as a child of the Father. Finally, the Spirit makes possible the resurrection to the life eternal. The activity of the Spirit in these two spheres can be outlined as follows:

In the Sphere of Creation

1. The Spirit of God goes forth to energize and bring created things into being.

2. The Spirit of God sustains the created beings at every moment.

3. The Spirit of God will be active in the bringing about of a new creation, a new heaven, and a new earth.

In the Sphere of Redemption

1. The Spirit of God regenerates the believer, bringing him or her into the spiritual family of God.

2. The Spirit of God empowers and sustains the life of the Christian believer as one grows in the grace of God.

3. The Spirit of God will bring about the final resurrection of the believer unto the life everlasting.

Three Epochs of the Spirit

Because God has revealed Himself in human history to accomplish His purpose of redemption, there is an important sequence to the activity of God's Spirit in the history of redemption. This is what I mean by an "epoch" of the Spirit: a period of redemptive history in which the activity of the Spirit was defined by certain historical limits, which were later changed in other periods of history.

Some people have called these historical periods "dispensations," and the most obvious ones are the Old Testament period and the New Testament period. It is clear that the Spirit could do things in the New Testament period, on the basis of the ministry and atoning work of Jesus, that He could not do in the Old Testament. But there is even a distinction in the New Testament between the activity of the Spirit in the life and ministry of Jesus, on the one hand, and the activity of the Spirit after the death, resurrection, and ascension of Jesus on the other hand. A comprehensive doctrine of the Holy Spirit must take into account these three successive epochs: in the Old Testament; in the life of Jesus; and in the church.

The Spirit in the Old Testament

The most obvious characteristic of the Spirit's activity in this first epoch is the apparent coming and going of the Spirit. He had no permanent location or dwelling place, and His personality was not as clearly defined as it was later. Just as Jesus gave us a clearer definition of the personality of the Father, so the personality of the Holy Spirit becomes clearer through the life of Jesus. Sometimes the power of the Spirit is confronted in the Old Testament as sheer terror, unqualified by the "grace and truth" which came in Jesus Christ. But the activity of the Holy Spirit in the Old Testament era is consistent with other periods in salvation history. The Spirit is active in creating and sustaining all things. Through the Spirit, God communicates with human beings. By the Spirit, God carries on His work of redemption.

The Spirit in Jesus

The most significant change in this second "epoch of the Spirit" is that during the earthly life of Jesus the Holy Spirit indwelt Jesus as He had never dwelt in any other person. Whereas Old Testament figures experienced a temporary visitation of the Spirit, Jesus was the embodiment of the Holy Spirit, who empowered all his miracles and ministry.

In addition, through the personality and moral character of Jesus, the Holy Spirit became more clearly defined in personal terms. Just as we know God as loving Father through the life and teaching of Jesus, we have come to know the Spirit as God's love in powerful action through Jesus. This second "epoch of the Spirit" could only come with the incarnation of the Son of God as Jesus of Nazareth. The incarnation was an event in history; it made a difference forevermore on how the Father relates to human beings. The incarnation also changed forever how the Spirit relates to human beings.

Because the Spirit indwelt Jesus in a special way, one's relationship to the Spirit is determined by his relationship to Jesus. Jesus could give the Holy Spirit to whom He willed. In the upper room to His disciples, or on the Day of Pentecost, the Holy Spirit came upon the believers through Jesus. Thus, Jesus is the incarnation of the Spirit and the Mediator of the Spirit to those who believe in Him.

The Spirit in the Church

The third "epoch of the Spirit" extends from the New Testament to the present time. This is why it would be incorrect to call this period the "New Testament Epoch of the Spirit." Also, this epoch did not begin with the beginning of the New Testament but with the resurrection and ascension of Jesus. From the upper room and the Day of Pentecost onward, the Holy Spirit has indwelt the church in a way that He has never indwelt any other group in all redemptive history. This is the power and glory of the church.

Jesus carries on His ministry through His body, the church, empowered by the Holy Spirit. This "epoch of the Spirit" will last until the Lord comes again to bring history to a close. The Spirit does not "come and go," as He did in the Old Testament period. Instead, He dwells in the body of the church and in the bodies of its individual members. This is an entirely new situation in redemptive history. No other group of people has ever had such a glorious commission or such enabling power to accomplish it as has the church of our Lord Jesus Christ, empowered by the Spirit.

The Relationships of the Spirit

A complete doctrine of the Holy Spirit requires not only a definition of His person, a description of His activity in the spheres of creation and redemption, and a consideration of the historical epochs of His activity but also an examination of His personal relationships. The most important of these are certainly His relationship to the Father, to the Son, and to believers.

The Spirit's Relationship to the Father

The most significant way of stating this relationship is to affirm the repeated biblical teaching that the Spirit is sent forth from the Father. Even if we think in Trinitarian terms and refer to the Spirit as fully personal God and to the Father as fully personal God, it still remains true that the functions of Father and Spirit are clearly distinguished. The Spirit is sent by the Father and proceeds from the Father. Never does the Spirit send the Father; nor does the Father proceed from the Spirit.

Since God is Spirit, how can the person of the Holy Spirit be distinguished in any way from this general definition of God as Spirit? An analogy of the sunlight and the sun might help our understanding of this mystery. The rays of the sun go forth from the ball of fire and light, which is their source; in one sense, they are continuous with the flaming sphere of the sun and not to be distinguished from it. Yet, the rays enter into plants, animals, rocks, and seas, setting in motion all kinds of activity that continue for awhile, even when the sun is hidden by a cloud or not visible at night. In a similar manner, the Spirit is God; but the Spirit is God going forth to create and redeem. If the Spirit remained only at the source and never went forth to create or redeem, there would never have been any creation or redemption or any Holy Spirit as He has been revealed in biblical history.

The Spirit, then, is God, even as the Father is God. But the Spirit is not the Father. Rather, the Father sends forth the Spirit to create and redeem. Even as the Son came not to do His own will, but the will of the Father, so the Spirit came not to do His own will, but the will of the Father. The only access to the Father is through the Spirit. The Spirit is God coming to us, communicating with us, redeeming us. The Spirit and the Father are One and the same God!

The Spirit's Relationship to the Son

The most significant way of stating this relationship is to remember Jesus' teaching that the Holy Spirit is sent in answer to His prayer and through His name (or Person) and that the ministry of the Spirit is to bear witness to Jesus. The Son is not the Source and Sender of the Spirit in the way that the Father is, but the Son is the Mediator through whom the Spirit comes, and the Son is the one to whom the Spirit bears witness.

The incarnation of the Son took place when the Holy Spirit overshadowed the virgin Mary. Thus, the Spirit is the instrument of the incarnation of the Son of God as Jesus of Nazareth. The Holy Spirit also empowered all the miracles and deeds of Jesus, raised Him from the dead, and descended upon the church to carry on the mission of Jesus in the world. The relationship of the Holy Spirit to the Son is so close that they can sometimes be identified. The Holy Spirit is called the Spirit of Christ. Yet, they can be clearly distinguished in their functions in redemptive history. Jesus the Son died on the cross, but the Spirit did not. Jesus returned to the "right hand" of the Father, but the Spirit did exactly the opposite. He came in power upon the believing disciples and promised to stay with them "forever."

The Spirit and Son have been with the Father from all eternity. The Spirit empowered the incarnate life and ministry of Jesus, raised Him from the dead, and continues the ministry of Jesus through His body the church. The Spirit draws believers to Christ and generates new spiritual life in them.

The Spirit's Relationship to Believers

The final relationship to be summarized in a comprehensive doctrine of the Holy Spirit is the relationship to believers. This relationship was clearly defined in our study of the biblical texts.

1. The Holy Spirit convicts and draws sinners to faith in Jesus Christ, generating new life in them so that they may become spiritual children of God. This is analogous to the activity of the Holy Spirit in creating physical breath and life. In the sphere of redemption, the Spirit gives new spiritual breath and life.

Some theologies have arisen in recent years that suggest that one may come to faith in Jesus and become a Christian without receiving the Holy Spirit. Then, at a later time, one may receive the "second blessing" or baptism of the Holy Spirit. Nothing could distort the biblical teaching more. Only by the convicting power of the Holy Spirit may one come to faith in Jesus. No one can be a Christian without the regenerating power of the Holy Spirit. Christians may receive later blessings and, hopefully, many fillings of the Spirit, but they cannot become Christians without the presence and power of the Holy Spirit.

2. The Holy Spirit continues to dwell in the life of the believers. The Spirit-Paraclete is God-with-us, God-within-us. The most intimate relationship we have with God is through the indwelling Spirit of God. Because the Spirit dwells in the body of believers as in a temple, the greatest purity of life and thought are expected. This indwelling Spirit is the basis and power of ethical conduct in the Christian life. It is also the witness and sign of our salvation. The presence

of the Holy Spirit in the life of the believer is the sign of one's salvation, the evidence that one is a child of God.

The indwelling Holy Spirit is also the basis of Christian unity. By His presence we love our brothers and sisters in the family of God. The Spirit makes us children of God; thereby, we become brothers and sisters in the same spiritual family.

3. The final activity of the Spirit will be to raise the believers in new spiritual bodies when Jesus comes again. Even as the Spirit raised Jesus from the dead, He will raise those who believe in Jesus at His second coming. The presence of the Holy Spirit in the life of the believers is the sign and seal of this coming victory over death in the resurrection of the dead. This final act of presenting us to the King will then make it possible for Jesus to deliver the kingdom to the Father that God may be "all and in all" (1 Cor. 15:24-28).

Such is the glorious activity of the Spirit of God from the first breath of creation to the triumph of the eternal kingdom of God. This is more than from "the cradle to the grave." This is the story of the whole sweep of God's creative and redemptive purpose from eternity to eternity, from the beginning of creation to the consummation of the ages!

10
The Holy Spirit Today

After an extensive study of the Holy Spirit in the Scriptures and a comprehensive statement of the doctrine of the Holy Spirit, an appropriate conclusion to our study is a consideration of the life and work of the Holy Spirit in our churches today. We have seen a dynamic revival of interest in the person and gifts of the Holy Spirit in recent years. Unfortunately, this renewal of interest has sometimes brought more bane than blessing. Churches have been torn asunder, pastors have been dismissed, and bitter conflict has been engendered among Christians.

The so-called "charismatic movement" has swept through churches of all denominations, emphasizing the *charismata,* or spiritual gifts, that are discussed in the Letters of Paul in the New Testament. Special emphasis has been placed on "tongues" or ecstatic speech, as a sign of the baptism of the Holy Spirit. The suggestion that one is not quite the Christian one ought to be without this gift has engendered strife and conflict. When tongues have broken out in public worship, it has further divided congregations and polarized sincere Christians. In the light of our study of the Spirit throughout the Bible and in Christian theology, let us consider these questions concerning the Spirit in our churches and in individual Christian lives today.

The Charismatic Movement Today

A wealth of literature has been published on the charismatic movement, and it would be inappropriate to try to summarize that vast body of literature here. However, from our study of the Holy Spirit in Scripture, and in the framework of Christian doctrine, it should be helpful to bring those insights to bear upon some of the problems in our churches today, as they deal with this strong new emphasis.

Speaking in Tongues

Nowhere in the Bible, in the original languages, does the expression "unknown tongues" exist. The word *"unknown"* was added by the King James translators to interpret the word *glossais,* which simply means "tongues," or languages. In the famous passage in Acts 2, on the Day of Pentecost, when the Holy Spirit was poured out upon the church, the disciples apparently spoke in languages of the countries around the Mediterranean Sea. The text says both that they spoke and heard in the languages in which they were born. This miracle fulfilled the promise of the baptism of the Spirit and empowered the church to witness to the gospel of Jesus Christ across the language barriers of their world.

However, in the church at Corinth (1 Cor. 12—14), the "tongues" which broke out in public worship seem to have been ecstatic or unintelligible speech. This is certainly the kind of phenomenon which characterizes the charismatic movement today. The speaker himself does not understand the sounds but usually emphasizes a feeling of the power and presence of the Lord in his life. This immediate experience of spiritual ecstasy has been the driving force of the charismatic movement.

Because the tongue speaking had created such confusion in the church at Corinth, Paul placed some very severe limitations upon the practice of tongues in public worship. Even though he did not reject them outright, Paul stated a strong preference for intelligent speech, desiring to speak even five words with understanding rather than ten thousand in a tongue (1 Cor. 14:19). Paul gave some very clear instructions on the control of tongues in public worship. If they had been followed carefully in our churches today, it is certain that much of the conflict regarding tongues would have been resolved. These are some of Paul's guidelines:

1. In the church it is preferable to speak intelligible words in order to build up the church (1 Cor. 14:4).

2. Desire the spiritual gift of prophecy, rather than tongues (v. 1). Prophecy is intelligible speech declaring the word of God.

3. Only two or three at most should be allowed to speak in a worship service and, then, only if they speak in turn and someone interprets in plain language so that the church may be edified.

4. If there is no interpretation, the tongue speakers should be silent (v.28).

5. Tongues may offend unbelievers and drive them further from the Lord, while prophecy will convict them and bring them to worship God (vv. 23-25).

The tongues phenomenon has been especially visible in the more structured liturgical churches. The spontaneity and enthusiasm which characterize the freer forms of worship already allows more room for ecstatic expression. The injunctions of Paul balance two factors, which must be kept in some kind of tension: do not quench the Spirit; and, yet, let all things be done decently and in order. If this balance can be maintained, the church will be edified.

Slain in the Spirit

Many of the frontier revivals in America were characterized by people getting the "barks" or "jerks" or sometimes by falling in a dead faint and remaining in that state for a period of time. This phenomenon is not limited to Christian revivalism; it can be seen in the ecstatic worship ceremonies of all religions and even in the excitement of festivals that are not religious at all.

Many of these experiences are analyzed by psychologists as outbursts of uncontrolled emotions, often stimulated by mass hysteria in great crowds. Yet, from the Old Testament through the New, the power of the Spirit to overwhelm human beings is quite clearly set forth, whether a Saul among the prophets or Ananias and Sapphira lying to the Spirit about their gift. These are warnings that the power of the Spirit is not something to be mocked or manipulated. The guidelines of Paul again would solve the problems. Let the mind be "fruitful," rather than inactive. Then the power of the Spirit can energize the mind and the emotions to do the work of the Lord in a constructive way. There are certainly times that the overwhelming joy of the presence of the Lord can carry us beyond our ability to speak or comprehend. But if such spiritual ecstasy is to edify the church and serve the cause of Christ, it must involve the mind, the body, and the spirit.

Demon Exorcisms

The Gospels record many examples of the casting out of demons or evil spirits among the miracles of Jesus. Some dismiss these as first-century explanations of mental illness and emotional disorders. The descriptions of the behavior of demon-possessed people do very closely resemble some types of mental illness; no doubt many of them would today be classified in medical terms.

Yet Jesus clearly identified the spiritual powers of the evil one as a threat to human well-being. Jesus Himself fought against the tempter, and the cries of the demon possessed were a challenge to His ministry. Paul spoke in more general terms of the "principalities and powers" that threaten our lives, but he appealed to us to live in the Spirit and be victorious over these forces. Paul did not exorcise demons in his ministry.

Obviously, two dangers loom before us as we consider the reality of the demonic powers today. On the one hand, we can be so sophisticated in our modern science that we dismiss any idea of Satan or the demonic entirely. On the other hand, we can become so obsessed with the demonic that we see demons in everybody and behind every bush. Satan wins a victory either way. The better way is to live in the power of the Holy Spirit, trusting God to deliver us from the forces which enslave us. From evil habits and spiritual forces that cripple our bodies and our souls, the power of God's Holy Spirit can deliver us. Preoccupation with the negative forces that threaten us, however real, can make it impossible to live the victorious Christian life.

Divine Healing

Another major emphasis in the charismatic movement today is upon physical and emotional healing. Surely all Christians believe that God is the Great Physician and that we should pray for healing and wholeness in our lives. But the line is crossed when people begin to focus on physical healing as more important than spiritual rebirth and when they suggest that if we have enough faith God will surely heal. The Bible is diametrically opposed to such a theology. God's power is sometimes demonstrated in the grace to bear physical pain and illness, rather than in removing it. Paul is a testimony to that. When people are made to bear the guilt of not having enough faith to heal themselves or their loved ones, their problem is only compounded.

Jesus refused to be forced into the role of simply being a divine healer. It would have diverted Him from His real mission as Savior and transformer of lives. This should be the clue for us. We should pray for physical and spiritual healing, but we should never try to manipulate people or God in order to accomplish our own purposes.

The Role of the Spirit in Our Lives Today

What is the role of the Holy Spirit in our churches, our evangelistic efforts, and in our individual lives today? The neglect of the biblical teaching about the activity of the Spirit in all aspects of our Christian lives has contributed to the distortions of the doctrine of the Holy Spirit that we see today.

Convicting by the Spirit

So many efforts are made today by often well-intentioned evangelists to get people saved and into the church that they seem to have forgotten that only the Holy Spirit can convict people of sin and bring them to Jesus. High-pressure tactics and programs wind up manipulating people and driving away the Spirit. We need more emphasis on the power of God and less emphasis upon human skills.

We need to pray for the Spirit's power to do what we cannot do—convict people of sin and draw them to Jesus. We must remind people to wait upon the Spirit and give Him opportunity to speak to hearts and touch lives. In our impatience we often run ahead of the Spirit and violate His freedom to convict and regenerate human lives.

Spirit-Directed Churches

The power of the Holy Spirit should be directing our churches in all that we do. Instead, we often plan a business meeting and then play politician by trying to round up enough votes to carry the motion we want to make. A congregation that is led by the Spirit will pray and consider an action until they come together in the mind of the Spirit and do His will, rather than their own.

A Spirit-directed church will pray and search for the Spirit's leadership in calling a pastor. Too many churches have campaigns in which one group tries to out vote the other, ensuring future conflict because they have followed their own will instead of the will of the Holy Spirit. A church is not a democracy, ruled by the majority of the members. It is a fellowship that strives to surrender itself to the rule of God's Spirit. Those who have had the privilege of being in such a spiritual fellowship can tell the difference between a Spirit-directed church and a people-directed church.

Missions in the Power of the Spirit

Many Christian groups have forsaken the missionary task entirely. They seem to feel that it is presumptuous for us, with all our problems in America, to try to convert people in other lands and other religions to Jesus Christ. We are not in the business of trying to convince people of the superiority of our American culture or our Christian religion. We are called by the Spirit to witness to Jesus Christ, and the Spirit takes over the task of convicting them and drawing them to Christ. To reject the missionary task is to reject the commission of our Lord and the call of the Spirit. To try to convert them to our culture or our religion is to prevent the work of the Holy Spirit in truly transforming their lives

Called by the Spirit

The Spirit of God, who called order and beauty out of the great deep in the work of creation, is now calling each of us to be His dwelling place and His instrument. He wants to think through our minds, speak through our lips, and work through our hands in this confused and broken world. The question is, Who is willing to offer his life to be the channel of the Spirit in His work of new creation and redemption?

Scripture Index